THE
=BEST=
BAR TRIVIA
BOOK EVER

THE BEST BAR TRIVIA BOOK EVER

ALL YOU NEED FOR PUB QUIZ DOMINATION

MICHAEL O'NEILL

Adamsmedia
Avon, Massachusetts

Published by
Adams Media, a division of F+W Media, Inc.
57 Littlefield Street, Avon, MA 02322. U.S.A.
www.adamsmedia.com

ISBN 10: 1-4405-7947-4
ISBN 13: 978-1-4405-7947-9
eISBN 10: 1-4405-7948-2
eISBN 13: 978-1-4405-7948-6

Printed in the United States of America.

10 9 8 7 6 5 4

Cover design by Jessica Pooler.

Cover images © _fla/123RF, iStockphoto.com/brightlady.
Interior images © 123RF.

This book is available at quantity discounts for bulk purchases.
For information, please call 1-800-289-0963.

ACKNOWLEDGMENTS

Thanks for the support of my family, friends, colleagues, and especially the trivia players who have supported my passion to entertain with information and musical accompaniment for so many years.

Special thanks go out to my wife, Julie; my parents, John and Carol; Matt and John Soldano; Amy Wrynn; Steve Morris; Alex Beuscher; Andy Cohen; Eric Farley; Kristin Glynn; Joel Bates; Dave Millar; Rob Chung; Phil Kliger; Alex Leonard; Bob Verdolino; Mike "Cutch" McCutcheon; John Doherty; Brett Erickson; Jim "The Jag" Varrichio; Chris Lawler; Elizabeth Steffen; Corey Rateau; Dan McCarthy; Ilya Rasner; W. Matt Sullivan; Matt Filipowicz; Marc Chamberland; Thomas Harte; Jim Weiss; John D'Amore; Brendan Sargent; Tom Hardej, Katie Corcoran Lytle; Dan "Mookie" Davis; Peter Newman; Stephen DiMarco; Dave and Beverly Robinson; Patrick McIntyre; Ally and Jake Eddy; Donohue's Bar & Grill; Elephant and Castle; T's Pub; and to Mike Breslau, for his significant contributions.

CONTENTS

THE FINAL ROUND 229

INTRODUCTION

Welcome to *The Best Bar Trivia Book Ever*. My name is Michael, and I'll be the trivia host guiding you through some of the most fascinating facts and stories from pop culture, academia, and more. If you've picked up this book, it's probably because you're a fan of a weekly pub quiz, and it's definitely because you're looking to up your game. After all, coming in at the middle of the pack every week isn't as fun as winning, especially when the top prize might be cash, money off your tab, or a gift certificate for next time. So buckle yourself in and get ready to learn some of the best facts so that you can come out on top.

I've been organizing Pop Quiz Team Trivia in Massachusetts and California for more than fifteen years, and I have collected and created more than 20,000 questions that have kept trivia enthusiasts guessing. In this book you will find the best and most interesting facts culled from my database, and from the inner reaches of my brain. The book is laid out just as I would organize a trivia night. The first three rounds are packed with popular categories like Business, Geography, Music, Vocabulary, and more. In each round I rank the facts by a value of 1, 3, 5, or 7 points, from easiest to most challenging. The final round offers a miscellany of more challenging trivia that can net you up to 20 points—if you're willing to take the risk.

What makes this book different than other trivia books is that this is the only one focused on the facts most commonly asked at pub quizzes. Here, we'll examine the origins of everyday things, the most, least, tallest, longest, smallest, shortest, youngest, and oldest of records, events, structures, people, and all things science. (Say it with me now: *Science!*) You'll get to know Oscar winners, captains of industry, world leaders, and troubled pop stars. If you memorize this book cover to cover, not only will you be more prepared than everyone else the next time you step foot into your neighborhood bar for your pub quiz, but you'll also save a ton of money on your tab when you win week after week. I hope you're ready, because we're about to start with Round 1 . . .

POP CULTURE

ROUND 1

MOVIES

Do you know . . .

- Which former teen star made her acting debut on a soap opera?
- What is the top grossing basketball movie of all time?
- Who is the only actor to have voiced characters in every Pixar movie?
- Who has won more Oscars than anyone else in history?
- What is the highest-grossing independent film to date?

If you don't know the answers to these questions, you should—and you will after you read through the facts in this chapter. You see, "Movies" is probably the single most popular pub quiz category, so the more trivia you know about this category, the better. Even so, it's easy to run into a "you know it or you don't" scenario when you're not familiar with the film in a question. But you can combat this by putting together a team with players of different ages, sexes, and interests to try to cover the widest number of movies. Studying up on your Best Picture Oscar winners also never hurts. So let's dive in and learn a little bit about the silver screen!

FILM DEBUTS
1 POINT

Will Ferrell had his first credited feature film role in *Austin Powers: International Man of Mystery* (1997).

∘°∘°∘∘

Twilight star **Kristen Stewart** made her film debut in *Panic Room* (2002), playing Jodie Foster's daughter.

∘°∘°∘∘

Lindsay Lohan first appeared on the soap opera *Another World* at age ten, and starred in two remakes for her first big screen roles in *The Parent Trap* (1998), and *Freaky Friday* (2003).

∘°∘°∘∘

Benicio del Toro played Duke, the Dog-Faced Boy in *Big Top Pee-wee* (1988), which was his first credited film role.

∘°∘°∘∘

Jon Hamm made his big screen debut as Young Pilot #2 in *Space Cowboys* (2000).

∘°∘°∘∘

Oscar nominee **Bradley Cooper** made his film debut in *Wet Hot American Summer* (2001).

°o°o°O°o

Leonardo DiCaprio was familiar to small-screen audiences thanks to his role on the final season of *Growing Pains*, but he made his film debut in the less than memorable *Critters 3* (1991), followed by a small part in *Poison Ivy* (1992). Four Oscar nominations later, I'd say he's recovered.

°o°o°O°o

Elijah Wood was first seen as Video-Game Boy #2 in *Back to the Future Part II* (1989).

°o°o°O°o

Hilary Swank had a part in the original *Buffy the Vampire Slayer* (1992). She went on to play unpopular roles in *The Next Karate Kid* (1994) and on *Beverly Hills, 90210* (1997–1998) . . . oh, and to win two Oscars for *Boys Don't Cry* (1999) and *Million Dollar Baby* (2004).

°o°o°O°o

Halle Berry, the runner-up in the 1986 Miss USA Competition, starred in Spike Lee's *Jungle Fever* (1991). Christy Fichtner, who won the 1986 Miss USA title, later starred in the reality show *Who Wants to Marry My Dad* (2003–2004).

°o°o°O°o

Ricki Lake got started playing Tracy Turnblad in John Waters's original *Hairspray* (1988). Lake was credited as Bridesmaid in *Working Girl* (1988) before landing a regular role as Holly Pelegrino on ABC's *China Beach*, and getting her own talk show in 1993.

The *Outsiders* (1983), based on the S.E. Hinton novel and directed by Francis Ford Coppola, featured an all-star cast of **C. Thomas Howell**, **Ralph Macchio**, **Matt Dillon**, **Rob Lowe**, **Patrick Swayze**, **Emilio Estevez**, **Tom Cruise**, and **Diane Lane** and launched the "Brat Pack" of the 1980s, which would later also include Molly Ringwald, Ally Sheedy, and Demi Moore.

Kevin Bacon made his film debut playing Chip Diller in *National Lampoon's Animal House* (1978). Bacon also played Jack in the original *Friday the 13th* (1980).

Paul Reubens, a.k.a. Pee-wee Herman, made his big-screen debut as Jake and Elwood's waiter in *The Blues Brothers* in 1980. The same year he served Cheech and Chong as the hotel desk clerk in *Cheech & Chong's Next Movie*.

Matthew Broderick and **Kiefer Sutherland** both made their debut in Neil Simon's *Max Dugan Returns* (1983). This is one of two films featuring both Kiefer and his father, Donald Sutherland. The other is *A Time to Kill* (1996).

BOX OFFICE HITS
3 POINTS

In 2013, *The Hunger Games: Catching Fire* became the first film in forty years with a female lead to become the highest grossing film of the year, beating out *Iron Man 3*. The previous film to do this was *The Exorcist* in 1973.

○°○°○°

Only two movies have grossed more than $2 billion worldwide, *Avatar* (2009) and *Titanic* (1997); both were directed by James Cameron.

○°○°○°

Frozen (2013) is the second top-grossing non-Pixar Disney cartoon film of all time in the United States, only behind *The Lion King* (1994). *The Lion King* is the top-grossing animated film of all time in the world, having made more than $1 billion at the global box office.

○°○°○°

The Hangover Part II (2011) had the biggest opening weekend in history for a comedy with nearly $86 million. Worldwide, it's the highest-grossing film in the trilogy, and has made more than half a billion dollars.

○°○°○°

The top grossing films of the 1980s were *E.T. the Extra-Terrestrial* (1982), *The Empire Strikes Back* (1980), *Return of the Jedi* (1983),

Batman (1989), *Raiders of the Lost Ark* (1981), and *Ghostbusters* (1984).

∘°₀°○∘

The highest grossing sports movies of all time are:
- Basketball—*Space Jam* (1996)
- Football—*The Blind Side* (2009)
- Baseball—*A League of Their Own* (1992)
- Hockey—*Miracle* (2004)
- Golf—*Tin Cup* (1996)
- Olympic Bobsledding—*Cool Runnings* (1993)

∘°₀°○∘

The highest-grossing movies by rating are:
- G—*The Lion King* (1994)
- PG—*Star Wars Episode I: The Phantom Menace* (1999)
- PG-13—*Avatar* (2009)
- R—*The Passion of the Christ* (2004)
- NC-17—*Showgirls* (1995)

∘°₀°○∘

The Hurt Locker (2008) is the lowest grossing film to ever win the Best Picture Academy Award.

∘°₀°○∘

Harry Potter, **Star Wars**, **James Bond**, and **Batman** are the highest-grossing movie franchises of all time in the United States.

Every movie has a tagline and some are more outrageous than others—and yes, they're all real. Keep these taglines in mind to take home a trivia win.

- *Alien³* (1992): "The bitch is back."
- *Armageddon* (1998): "Earth. It was fun while it lasted."
- *The Big Lebowski* (1998): "Her life was in their hands. Now her toe is in the mail."
- *Catch Me If You Can* (2002): "The true story of a real fake."
- *Dazed and Confused* (1993): "See it with a bud."
- *Edward Scissorhands* (1990): "His story will touch you, even though he can't."
- *Fight Club* (1999): "Mischief. Mayhem. Soap."
- *Finding Nemo* (2003): "There are 3.7 trillion fish in the ocean. They're looking for one."
- *The Fly* (1986): "Be afraid. Be very afraid."
- *The Graduate* (1967): "This is Benjamin. He's a little worried about his future."
- *Office Space* (1999): "Work sucks."
- *The Royal Tenenbaums* (2001): "Family isn't a word . . . It's a sentence."
- *There's Something about Mary* (1998): "Love is in the hair."
- *This Is Spinal Tap* (1984): "Does for rock and roll what *The Sound of Music* did for hills."
- *Wayne's World* (1992): "You'll laugh, you'll cry, you'll hurl."

Bridesmaids (2011) is the highest-grossing R-rated female comedy of all time, bumping ***Sex and the City*** (2008) into second place.

○ °○° ○ ○

Inglourious Basterds (2009) is Quentin Tarantino's highest-grossing film to date, earning eight Oscar nominations and more than $320 million. In case spelling counts at your next pub quiz, remember that both words in the title are spelled incorrectly.

○ °○° ○ ○

My Big Fat Greek Wedding (2002) never reached number one at the box office, but it is the highest-grossing romantic comedy of all time and was highest-grossing independent film until it was surpassed by *The Passion of the Christ* (2004).

○ °○° ○ ○

Transformers: Revenge of the Fallen (2009) is the highest-grossing film ever released on a Wednesday.

○ °○° ○ ○

Independence Day (1996) is the highest-grossing film to star an African American (Will Smith) in the lead role.

○ °○° ○ ○

During a seven-day period in November 1994, Tim Allen simultaneously starred in the highest-grossing film in the United States (***The Santa Clause***), topped the *New York Times* bestseller list (*Don't*

Stand Too Close to a Naked Man), and starred on TV's top-rated show (*Home Improvement*).

≡ ANIMATION ≡
5 POINTS

John Ratzenberger is the only person to voice a character in every single Pixar film.

○ ° ○ ° ○ ○

The Incredibles (2004) was the first PG-rated movie released by Pixar, and ***Up*** (2009) was the second.

○ ° ○ ° ○ ○

Snow White and the Seven Dwarfs (1937) was the first full-length Disney animated feature film.

○ ° ○ ° ○ ○

Sleeping Beauty (1959) features the most onscreen consumption of alcohol, with 2 minutes and 56 seconds in total.

○ ° ○ ° ○ ○

The Pixar film ***Shrek*** (2001) is loosely based on William Steig's 1990 picture book, *Shrek!*.

○ ° ○ ° ○ ○

Three animated films have been nominated for Best Picture: **Beauty and the Beast** (1991), **Up** (2009), and **Toy Story 3** (2010).

∘°○°○∘

The British team of Wallace and Gromit has appeared in four short films in total and only one feature: **Wallace & Gromit: The Curse of the Were-Rabbit** (2005).

∘°○°○∘

An uncredited Kathleen Turner provided the speaking voice of Jessica Rabbit in **Who Framed Roger Rabbit** (1988). The film also contains the longest onscreen credits for any film.

∘°○°○∘

Mickey Mouse and Minnie Mouse debuted in the film **Steamboat Willie** (1928). It's the first animated short with synchronized sound.

∘°○°○∘

Mae Questel, who plays Aunt Bethany in **National Lampoon's Christmas Vacation** (1989), provided the voice of Betty Boop in more than 150 animated shorts, and provided the voice of *Popeye*'s Olive Oyl for more than twenty years, starting in the 1930s.

∘°○°○∘

Labyrinth (1983), directed by Jim Henson, produced by George Lucas, and starring David Bowie and Jennifer Connelly, features a CGI (computer-generated imagery) owl during the title sequence. This was the first attempt at a photo-realistic CGI animal ever in a feature film.

∘°∘°∘°

In 1972, **Fritz the Cat**, based on a comic strip by Robert Crumb, was the first animated film to ever receive an X rating. It's also the most successful independent animated film of all time, grossing nearly $200 million worldwide.

∘°∘°∘°

The Annie Awards have been given out by the International Animated Film Society every year since 1972. **How to Train Your Dragon** (2010), **The Incredibles** (2004), **Kung Fu Panda** (2008), and **Wallace & Gromit: The Curse of the Were-Rabbit** (2005) are tied for the record for most nominations—with sixteen apiece. (Each took home ten awards.)

∘°∘°∘°

The soundtracks to **Cinderella** (1950), **The Lion King** (1994), **Pocahontas** (1995), **Curious George** (2006), and **Frozen** (2013) all reached #1 on the *Billboard* 200 list.

═══ THE OSCARS ═══
7 POINTS

Walt Disney received a record twenty-six Oscars and fifty-nine nominations. **Mary Poppins** (1964) is the only film he produced that was nominated for Best Picture.

At 224 minutes, **Gone with the Wind** (1939) is the longest movie ever to win Best Picture.

∘°₀°∘

Italy has won Foreign Language category more times than any other country—a total of thirteen times.

∘°₀°∘

In 1998, playing Queen Elizabeth I earned Judi Dench the Best Supporting Actress Oscar for **Shakespeare in Love** and Cate Blanchett the Best Actress nomination for **Elizabeth**.

∘°₀°∘

Meryl Streep has received the most Academy Award nominations (eighteen) for an actress, winning three.

∘°₀°∘

Jack Nicholson has the most Academy Award nominations for an actor with twelve.

∘°₀°∘

Paul Newman portrayed the character Fast Eddie Felson twice, twenty-five years apart, in **The Hustler** (1961) and in **The Color of Money** (1986), for which he earned his only acting Oscar award.

In 1998, **Roberto Benigni** (*Life is Beautiful*) became the second man to direct himself to a Best Actor Oscar. Laurence Olivier (*Hamlet*, 1948) was the first.

∘°ₒ°O∘

Paul Haggis is the only person to write back-to-back Best Picture Oscar winners: *Million Dollar Baby* (2004) and *Crash* (2005).

∘°ₒ°O∘

Alfred Hitchcock never won an Oscar for Best Director, and his only film to win Best Picture was *Rebecca* (1940).

∘°ₒ°O∘

Joan Fontaine became the only person to win an Oscar for acting in a Hitchcock film when she won Best Actress for *Suspicion* (1941).

∘°ₒ°O∘

Best Picture Oscar winner **_The Departed_** (2006) drops the f-bomb 237 times. Martin Scorsese beat that with the Best Picture–nominated **_The Wolf of Wall Street_** (2013), which has more than 500 f-bombs.

∘°ₒ°O∘

John Cazale, who died in 1978, only appeared in five movies, all of which were nominated for Best Picture: *The Godfather* (1972), *The Conversation* (1974), *The Godfather: Part II* (1974), *Dog Day Afternoon* (1975), and *The Deer Hunter* (1978).

∘°∘°∘°∘

Billy Bob Thornton won the Best Adapted Screenplay Oscar for *Sling Blade* (1996), which he also starred in and directed.

∘°∘°∘°∘

Sean Connery is the only James Bond actor to go on and win an Oscar. He won Best Actor in a Supporting Role for *The Untouchables* (1987).

∘°∘°∘°∘

There have been three sports-based movies that have won the Best Picture Oscar award: ***Rocky*** (1976), ***Chariots of Fire*** (1981), and ***Million Dollar Baby*** (2005).

∘°∘°∘°∘

Fast Times at Ridgemont High (1982) features three future Oscar winners: Nicolas Cage (*Leaving Las Vegas*, 1995), Sean Penn (*Mystic River*, 2003 and *Milk*, 2008), and Forest Whitaker (*Last King of Scotland,* 2006).

Actors don't always get to choose what their final film will be, and in some (but not all) cases it can be one of their least remarkable or their most memorable. But in bar trivia, everything is fair game, so it's good to have a working knowledge of a few final films—both good and bad.

- Marilyn Monroe and Clark Gable: *The Misfits* (1961)
- Paul Newman: *The Meerkats* (2008)
- Elvis Presley: *Change of Habit* (1969)
- Bob Hope: *Spies Like Us* (1985)
- Humphrey Bogart: *The Harder They Fall* (1956)
- Chris Farley: *Almost Heroes* (1998)
- John Belushi: *Neighbors* (1981)
- Spencer Tracy: *Guess Who's Coming to Dinner* (1967)
- Marlon Brando: *The Score* (2001)
- John Wayne: *The Shootist* (1976)
- Audrey Hepburn: *Always* (1989)
- Ronald Reagan: *The Killers* (1964)
- Grace Kelly: *High Society* (1956)
- John Candy: *Canadian Bacon* (1995)
- Brandon Lee: *The Crow* (1994)

CHAPTER 2

MUSIC

Do you know . . .

- What band was originally called Mookie Blaylock?
- How many copies does an album need to sell to be certified Gold?
- Who was the first Beatle to release a solo album?
- Who has performed more concerts in Madison Square Garden than any other artist?
- What's the longest song to reach #1 on the charts?

If you're not sure, you're in the right place. Here you'll learn the answers to these questions, and more! In addition to learning all the facts in this chapter, you can also up your music round game by:

1. Always paying attention to what song is playing when you're walking through any public space. See if you can name the tune and artist in fewer than ten seconds. If not, either Shazam it, or look it up later.
2. Spending a little time looking through the *Billboard* Hot 100 charts to bone up on #1 singles.
3. Picking a band or bands you like and reading for five minutes about them online to try to find one interesting fact to share

later. It's much easier to remember facts you like and that you repeat.

If all else fails, just stick to the "One-Hit Wonders." After all, "Pac-Man Fever" is, by any measure, one of the worst songs ever recorded, but it sure made Buckner & Garcia a lot of money. And "Gangnam Style" will always be the first song to grab two billion views on You-Tube.

MUSICAL DEBUTS

1 POINT

England's Newest Hit Makers is the title of the Rolling Stones debut album in 1964.

∘°∘°○∘

George Harrison was the first member of The Beatles to release a solo album: ***All Things Must Pass*** (1970). George Harrison lost a copyright infringement suit over the song "My Sweet Lord" on his solo album because it sounded a bit too much like The Chiffons's "He's So Fine."

∘°∘°○∘

Lady Gaga, born Stefani Joanne Angelina Germanotta, earned six Grammy nominations for her debut album, ***The Fame*** (2008). Lady Gaga took her stage name from the Queen song, "Radio Ga Ga" (1984).

∘°∘°○∘

Katy Perry's debut album was titled ***Katy Hudson*** (2001), which uses her actual last name. The genre is Christian rock, which may be a bit different from the genre of albums she releases these days.

∘°∘°○∘

Lady Antebellum made their debut in 2007 as guest vocalists on Jim Brickman's single "**Never Alone**."

°O°O°

Gorillaz's 2001 debut album sold more than seven million copies, and the band earned an entry in *The Guinness Book of World Records* as the Most Successful Virtual Band.

°O°O°

The **certification thresholds** for albums are:

- Silver—100,000
- Gold—500,000
- Platinum—1,000,000
- Diamond—10,000,000

°O°O°

Linkin Park debuted with the album ***Hybrid Theory***, which was certified Diamond in 2005.

°O°O°

In 2005, with **"Run It!,"** Chris Brown became the first male artist to have his debut single top the *Billboard* singles chart since Montell Jordan's "This is How We Do It" (1995).

°O°O°

"I Don't Want to Miss a Thing" (1998) is the only Aerosmith song that debuted at number one. Diane Warren wrote the song for Celine Dion, but she turned it down.

°O°O°

The Piper at the Gates of Dawn (1967) is Pink Floyd's debut album. It is the only album made under the leadership of Syd Barrett, who left the band in 1968. "Wish You Were Here" and "Shine On You Crazy Diamond" are tributes to Barrett.

₀°₀°O₀

Pearl Jam originally called itself Mookie Blaylock, after the National Basketball Association (NBA) player, but changed their name when they signed to Epic Records. Their debut album, ***Ten*** (1991), is titled for Blaylock's jersey number.

₀°₀°O₀

Thomas Dolby's debut album is titled ***The Golden Age of Wireless*** (1982). "She Blinded Me with Science" from that album reached #5 on the *Billboard* Hot 100, and will forever be remembered as the song that makes everyone yell *"Science!"* when playing pub trivia.

₀°₀°O₀

Greetings from Asbury Park (1973) is Bruce Springsteen's debut album. "Blinded by the Light" was its first single, but this song is better known by Manfred Mann's Earth Band cover version. Manfred Mann changed the lyric "cut loose like a deuce" to "revved up like a deuce," which is commonly misheard as "wrapped up like a douche."

₀°₀°O₀

Cyndi Lauper became the first female singer to have four top-five *Billboard* Hot 100 hits off a single album, her debut ***She's So Unusual***

(1983). The hits are "Girls Just Want to Have Fun," "Time After Time," "She Bop," "All Through the Night," and "Money Changes Everything."

═══ ON TOUR ═══
3 POINTS

In August of 1967, **Jimi Hendrix** was booed off the stage when opening for The Monkees. The Monkees had two number-one hits, and Hendrix lasted only six shows of the tour.

○°○°○○

George Harrison and Ravi Shankar, who is Norah Jones's father, organized **The Concert for Bangladesh** at Madison Square Garden on August 1, 1971. The recording of the concert won the 1973 Grammy for Album of the Year.

○°○°○○

Paul McCartney filled in for Kurt Cobain during a Nirvana reunion at **12-12-12: The Concert for Sandy Relief**.

○°○°○○

Up with People has performed at the most **Super Bowl** halftime shows (four). Bruno Mars and Red Hot Chili Peppers performed at the most-watched halftime show in history in 2014.

○°○°○○

Elton John has performed more concerts in Madison Square Garden than any other artist, performing his sixtieth on his sixtieth birthday.

∘°ₒ°O∘

Tim McGraw and Faith Hill's 2006–2007 **Soul2Soul II Tour** became the highest-grossing country music tour in history.

∘°ₒ°O∘

Queen's performance at the 1985 **Live Aid** concert was voted the best live rock performance of all time in a 2005 industry poll.

∘°ₒ°O∘

Phil Collins flew across the Atlantic on the Concorde in order to play sets at both the **London and Philadelphia Live Aid** concerts in 1985.

∘°ₒ°O∘

Austin City Limits first aired in 1976, and has become American television's longest-running concert music program.

∘°ₒ°O∘

Though they would perform together one more time on the rooftop of Apple Corps in 1969, The Beatles played their last official concert at **Candlestick Park** in San Francisco on August 29, 1966.

Think all those songs you know and love were original? Not so fast! Many of the most popular (and strangely catchy) songs are actually covers. Swallow your disappointment as you see whose music you *really* love.

- Eric Clapton covered Bob Marley's "I Shot the Sheriff"
- No Doubt covered Talk Talk's "It's My Life"
- The Byrds covered Bob Dylan's "Mr. Tambourine Man"
- Sheryl Crow covered Cat Stevens's "The First Cut Is the Deepest"
- Bow Wow Wow covered The Strangeloves's "I Want Candy"
- Nazareth covered The Everly Brothers's "Love Hurts"
- Bananarama covered Shocking Blue's "Venus"
- Whitney Houston covered Dolly Parton's "I Will Always Love You"
- The Fugees covered Roberta Flack's "Killing Me Softly"
- Ike and Tina Turner covered Creedence Clearwater Revival's "Proud Mary"
- Aretha Franklin covered Otis Redding's "Respect"
- Sinead O'Connor covered Prince's "Nothing Compares 2 U"
- Dropkick Murphys covered Woody Guthrie's "I'm Shipping Up to Boston"
- Green Day covered John Lennon's "Working Class Hero"
- Aretha Franklin covered Carole King's "(You Make Me Feel Like) A Natural Woman"

The Who was listed as the loudest band by *The Guinness Book of World Records* in 1976, playing at 126 decibels at **The Valley** stadium, Charlton, London, England.

∘°∘°O∘

U2's **360 Tour** (2009–2011) is the most profitable tour of all time, earning $736 million, with more than seven million people in attendance.

∘°∘°O∘

Perry Farrell originally conceived the music festival **Lollapalooza** as a farewell tour for his band, Jane's Addiction.

∘°∘°O∘

Debuting in 2002, the **Bonnaroo Music Festival** is held annually in Tennessee.

∘°∘°O∘

In 1993, Pearl Jam performed at the **Empire Polo Club** in California for 25,000 fans as part of a boycott of Ticketmaster-controlled venues. Six years later the venue became the home of Coachella . . . which today is serviced by Ticketmaster.

∘°∘°O∘

South by Southwest (SXSW), a set of music and film festivals, was founded in 1987. It has grown into one of the largest music festivals in the United States, attracting 15,000 to 20,000 visitors a year.

°o°O°o°

Ritchie Havens was the first act to perform at **Woodstock** on Friday, August 15, 1969. Jimi Hendrix was the last. Hendrix played from 9 A.M. until 11:10 A.M. on Monday, August 18.

BESTSELLING ARTISTS
5 POINTS

Bryan Adams is the bestselling Canadian rock artist in history. He has sold more than sixty-five million albums worldwide.

°o°O°o°

Celine Dion had nine bestselling French albums before recording her first in English in 1990. She is the bestselling Canadian artist of all time, and the first Canadian to win the Record of the Year Grammy in 1999.

°o°O°o°

Selling more than thirty million albums worldwide, **Whitney Houston**'s self-titled debut in 1985 is the bestselling debut album of any artist. *The Bodyguard* (1992) is the bestselling movie soundtrack.

°o°O°o°

George Benson recorded the first million-selling jazz album in 1976, *Breezin'*.

○ °○° ○ ○

Tammy Wynette was the first female country singer to earn a Platinum album with *Tammy's Greatest Hits* (1969).

○ °○° ○ ○

Julio Iglesias is the bestselling Latin music artist of all time, having sold more than 300 million records worldwide.

○ °○° ○ ○

Shania Twain recorded the bestselling country album of all time, *Come On Over* (1997).

○ °○° ○ ○

Hall and Oates are the world's bestselling singing music duo, recording six #1 hits: "Rich Girl," "Kiss on My List," "Private Eyes," "I Can't Go for That (No Can Do)," "Maneater," and "Out of Touch."

○ °○° ○ ○

Peter Frampton, former guitarist for the band Humble Pie, recorded the highest-selling album of 1976 as a solo artist with *Frampton Comes Alive!* It was the bestselling live album for decades, and to date has been certified Platinum eight times.

○ °○° ○ ○

Don McLean's "American Pie" (1971) is the longest song to reach #1 on the charts at eight minutes, thirty-two seconds. The song commemorates the 1959 plane crash that took the lives of Buddy Holly, Ritchie Valens, and the Big Bopper (J.P. Richardson).

○°○°○°

Maurice Williams and the Zodiacs's "Stay" is the shortest tune ever to reach #1 on the charts at one minute, thirty-seven seconds.

○°○°○°

Eminem is the bestselling hip-hop artist of all time, having sold more than 100 million albums.

○°○°○°

Since 1991, there have been nineteen albums that have sold more than 1 million copies in their first week. **Taylor Swift** is the only female artist who has released two of them. After Aretha Franklin and Madonna, Swift is the only female singer to chart more than forty Top 40 hits.

BAND NAME ORIGINS
7 POINTS

The Beatles's name was inspired by Buddy Holly's band, The Crickets. The "Beat" in the band's name was intended to be a musical pun.

The **Rolling Stones** got their band name from a 1950 Muddy Waters's song, "Rollin' Stone."

∘°∘°O∘

The Killers got their name from the New Order video for "Crystal." The Killers was the name of the fictional band in the video as featured on the bass drum.

∘°∘°O∘

The alternative rock band **311** is named for the police code for indecent exposure in Omaha, Nebraska. The name was chosen after the band's original guitarist was arrested for skinny dipping in a public pool.

∘°∘°O∘

Radiohead took their name from the Talking Heads song "Radio Head."

∘°∘°O∘

Toad the Wet Sprocket got their name from a Monty Python sketch that made fun of silly band names.

∘°∘°O∘

Pink Floyd took their name from the first names of two blues musicians, whose last names are Anderson and Council, respectively.

○ °₀° O ○

Eve 6 got their name from a cloning episode on *The X-Files*. The show was about ten clones of a girl named Eve. The sixth clone was a crazy psycho.

○ °₀° O ○

After seeing a miscaptioned photo of W.C. Fields, the **Gin Blossoms** chose their name from the old slang term for burst capillaries on the face of someone who drank too much for too many years.

○ °₀° O ○

Smash Mouth took their name from a football term coined by Chicago Bears coach Mike Ditka.

○ °₀° O ○

Led Zeppelin took their name from an insult made by The Who's drummer, Keith Moon. He said that "they'd go over like a lead balloon."

○ °₀° O ○

UB40 got their name from the code number on the British unemployment benefit card.

○ °₀° O ○

Nickelback was named by member Mike Kroeger, who at the time worked at Starbucks. He would commonly say to customers, "Here's your nickel back."

○ºₒºO○

Lynyrd Skynyrd is named for the band members' high school gym teacher in Jacksonville, Florida.

○ºₒºO○

ABBA, **'N Sync**, and **TLC** each took their band names from the initials of their members.

○ºₒºO○

Steely Dan got its name from a strap-on dildo referenced in William S. Burroughs's book *Naked Lunch.*

=== **"YOU'RE SO VAIN"** ===

In November 1972, Carly Simon released the song "You're So Vain" off her album *No Secrets*, and there has been speculation ever since about who exactly she was singing about. Was it Mick Jagger, who sang backup vocals on the song? Warren Beatty? David Geffen? Her ex-husband, James Taylor? If you want to know the truth, it could cost you. Simon whispered the name of the famed suitor into the ear of NBC Sports president, Dick Ebersol, who won the top bid at a charity auction for $50,000.

TELEVISION

Do you know . . .

- Who was the original host of *The Tonight Show*?
- Which singing competition is a remake of a Dutch show that debuted in 2010?
- What was the most-watched series finale of all time?
- What city hosted MTV's first *The Real World*?
- Who was the oldest person to guest host Saturday Night Live?

If you don't know how to answer these questions, don't worry. This chapter will reveal everything you need to know about iconic TV. It doesn't matter if you grew up with *The Brady Bunch*, *Cheers*, *Friends*, or *Breaking Bad*; you can enjoy learning about the shows that came before you by using TV Land, Netflix, and Hulu to help fill in the gaps. So, if a friend asks you to binge-watch *Gilligan's Island*, do it. You may need those theme song lyrics some day (and the good news/bad news is that you will never get them out of your head again).

TELEVISION FIRSTS

1 POINT

Steve Allen was the first host of *The Tonight Show*, from 1954 to 1957. Jack Paar bridged the gap to Johnny Carson, who, after thirty years behind the desk, passed the torch to Jay Leno. Conan O'Brien hosted briefly in 2009 and 2010, and Jimmy Fallon took over in 2014.

○ ○ ○ ○ ○

On October 11, 1996, *The X-Files* aired the episode "**Home**," the first show on network television in America to receive a viewer discretion warning for graphic content.

○ ○ ○ ○ ○

New York was the first city to host the seven strangers of MTV's *The Real World* in 1992. Twenty-nine seasons later, it's one of the longest-running reality series of all time. *Cops* is the longest, debuting in 1989.

○ ○ ○ ○ ○

Instant replay was first employed during the telecast of the Army-Navy football game on December 7, 1963.

○ ○ ○ ○ ○

In 2008, **Jeff Probst** of *Survivor* became the first winner of the Emmy award for Outstanding Host for a Reality or Reality-Competition Program, and then won three more times after.

∘°o°O∘

60 Minutes was the first network TV show without theme music, if you don't count the ticking clock.

∘°o°O∘

The Flintstones (1960–1966) is regarded as the first primetime animated series, and it was the most successful until *The Simpsons* came around in 1989.

∘°o°O∘

The **first interracial kiss** on American television occurred on an episode of *Star Trek* ("Plato's Stepchildren," 1968). Captain Kirk kissed Lt. Uhura.

∘°o°O∘

Here's the first time audiences heard **swear words** on TV:
- Hell—*Star Trek*, 1967
- Goddammit—*All in the Family*, 1971
- Son-of-a-bitch—*MASH*, 1973
- Fuck—*Saturday Night Live*, 1981
- Shit—*Chicago Hope*, 1999

∘°∘°O∘

The first televised **presidential debate** was between Richard Nixon and John F. Kennedy. It took place on September 26, 1960.

∘°∘°O∘

The first white artist to perform on ***Soul Train*** was Elton John, who sang "Mama Can't Buy You Love" in 1979.

∘°∘°O∘

The first black actor to star in a TV series was **Bill Cosby** on *I Spy* (1965–1968).

∘°∘°O∘

Billy Crystal portrayed the first openly gay character on primetime television, as Jodie Dallas on *Soap* (1977–1981).

∘°∘°O∘

The first time a **toilet** was heard flushing on primetime television was on *All in the Family*, on January 12, 1971.

SATURDAY NIGHT LIVE

3 POINTS

Saturday Night Live (*SNL*), which debuted in 1975, has the most primetime **Emmy awards** of any show with thirty-seven, and the most nominations with 156.

₀°₀°O°

The first sports personality to host *Saturday Night Live* was **Fran Tarkenton**, and the first comedian was **George Carlin**. The first musical guest was **Billy Preston**.

₀°₀°O°

Don Pardo has been the announcer for *Saturday Night Live* since its debut.

₀°₀°O°

Dennis Miller hosted Weekend Update for the longest period: six years.

₀°₀°O°

At seven years old, **Drew Barrymore** was the youngest person to ever host *SNL*, in 1982. With six appearances, she is also the most frequent female host, a record previously held by Candice Bergen.

₀°₀°O°

The oldest person to guest host *Saturday Night Live* was **Betty White**, who was eighty-eight years old when she hosted in 2010.

∘°ₒ°O∘

Chris Elliott's daughter Abby was the first second-generation cast member and the youngest female cast member when she joined the show in 2008 at twenty-one years of age. **Anthony Michael Hall**, who joined the cast for one season in 1985, was the youngest cast member at age seventeen.

∘°ₒ°O∘

John Candy appeared in ten films with *SNL* alumni, more than any other non-*SNL* cast member.

∘°ₒ°O∘

The first German-speaking host of *Saturday Night Live* was **Christoph Waltz**, who won Oscars for *Inglourious Basterds* (2009) and *Django Unchained* (2012).

∘°ₒ°O∘

George Wendt of *Cheers* fame is the uncle of *SNL* cast member Jason Sudeikis.

∘°ₒ°O∘

Kenan Thompson, born in 1978, was the first cast member of *SNL* to be younger than the show itself.

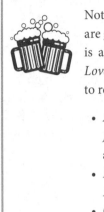

Not all spinoff series are created equal. Some spinoffs are good, some are not-so-good. For every *Frasier*, there is a *Joey*. For every *Family Matters*, there is a *Joanie Loves Chachi*. For better or worse, here are a few spinoffs to remember.

- *All in the Family* inspired *Maude*, *Good Times*, *The Jeffersons*, *Checking In*, *Archie Bunker's Place*, *Gloria*, and *704 Hauser*
- *Beverly Hills, 90210* inspired *Melrose Place*, *Models, Inc.*, *JAG*, and *NCIS*
- *Cheers* inspired *Frasier*
- *Dallas* inspired *Knots Landing*
- *Diff'rent Strokes* inspired *The Facts of Life*
- *Love, American Style* inspired *Happy Days*
- *Happy Days* inspired *Laverne and Shirley*, *Blansky's Beauties*, *Mork and Mindy*, *Out of the Blue*, and *Joanie Loves Chachi*
- *Perfect Strangers* inspired *Family Matters*
- *16 and Pregnant* inspired *Teen Mom*
- *The Tracey Ullman Show* inspired *The Simpsons*

The **"More Cowbell"** sketch starring Will Ferrell and guest host Christopher Walken centered around the fictional recording of Blue Öyster Cult's "(Don't Fear) The Reaper."

○ °○° ○ ○

Darrell Hammond holds the record for saying "Live from New York, it's Saturday Night" more times than any other cast member. Chevy Chase was the first to say it in 1975.

≡ REALITY CHECK ≡
5 POINTS

Survivor is based on the Swedish show *Expedition Robinson*.

∘ᵒ∘ᵒ∘

MTV's **The Real World** was inspired by the 1973 PBS documentary series *An American Family*.

∘ᵒ∘ᵒ∘

The Voice is a remake of a Dutch show that debuted in 2010.

∘ᵒ∘ᵒ∘

The Amazing Race won nine of the first ten Primetime Emmy Awards for Outstanding Reality-Competition Program, starting in 2003. *Top Chef* broke the streak in 2010.

∘ᵒ∘ᵒ∘

Alana Thompson is a pageant contestant on **Here Comes Honey Boo Boo**. Her family gained attention on the TLC series *Toddlers & Tiaras*. The series takes place in and around McIntyre, Georgia.

Kesha's family hosted Paris Hilton and Nicole Richie on a 2005 episode of *The Simple Life*.

∘°∘°O∘

FX's *Nip/Tuck*, created by Ryan Murphy, inspired the creation of the reality show *Dr. 90210*.

∘°∘°O∘

 Julie Chen has been the host of CBS's *Big Brother* since its debut in 2000.

∘°∘°O∘

Pawn Stars centers on the Harrison family pawn shop in Las Vegas. In 2011, *Pawn Stars* was the highest-rated series on History (formerly known as The History Channel), and the #2 reality series behind *Jersey Shore*.

∘°∘°O∘

Centered on the Robertson family in West Monroe, Louisiana, A&E's *Duck Dynasty*'s fourth season became the most watched nonfiction cable series in history with more than eleven million viewers.

∘°∘°O∘

Donnie Wahlberg from New Kids on the Block (NKOTB) is the executive producer of the documentary series *Boston's Finest* on TNT, and is featured along with his brothers Mark and Paul Wahlberg on the 2014 reality show *Wahlburgers*, which is based on the restaurant they own together.

○ °○° O ○

Dave Navarro, former guitarist for Jane's Addiction and the Red Hot Chili Peppers, is host of Spike TV's **Ink Master**.

○ °○° O ○

Cake Boss (TLC), which premiered in 2009, features Buddy Valastro at work in Hoboken, New Jersey.

○ °○° O ○

Project Runway made Tim Gunn a star, and popularized his catch-phrase: "Make It Work."

○ °○° O ○

Omarosa Manigault, the original villain of **The Apprentice**, is the only contestant to compete in three seasons. She did not make it to the finals on any of them.

FINALES
7 POINTS

"Fabulous" is the last word spoken in the final episode of **Sex and the City**.

With more than 100 million viewers, the most watched series finale of all time was **M*A*S*H** (aired February 28, 1983).

"Good Riddance (Time of Your Life)" plays in the final scene of **Seinfeld**. Journey's "Don't Stop Believin'" plays during the last moments of **The Sopranos**.

Airing during day two of the 1992 Los Angeles riots, the series finale of **The Cosby Show** had more than forty-four million viewers on April 30, 1992.

Janeane Garofalo played Paul and Jamie's grown daughter, Mabel Buchman, on the final episode of **Mad about You**.

Leslie Nielsen played Lucas, Blanche's uncle who married Dorothy, in the final episode of **The Golden Girls**.

Bette Midler was the final guest on **The Tonight Show Starring Johnny Carson** (May 21, 1992).

COMMERCIALS

Commercials are rife with "Before They Were Stars" stories, and here are a few of the celebrities who hawked products in TV ads before making the big time.

- Jason Alexander: McDonald's
- Tim Allen: Mr. Goodwrench
- Courteney Cox: Tampax
- Bryan Cranston: Preparation H
- Leonardo DiCaprio: Bubble Yum
- Demi Moore: Diet Coke
- Brad Pitt: Pringles
- Keanu Reeves: Corn Flakes
- Paul Rudd: Super Nintendo
- Bruce Willis: Seagram's

Billy Crystal was both the first and last guest on **The Tonight Show with Jay Leno**.

∘°ₒ°○∘

During the last six minutes of the **Six Feet Under** series finale, as Claire Fisher (played by Lauren Ambrose) drives away, we fast-forward to see how each of the main characters dies, while Sia's "Breathe Me" plays.

∘°ₒ°○∘

"Quiet!" is the only word ever uttered by Darryl and Darryl, when they screamed at their wives on the final episode of *Newhart*.

∘°∘°○∘

Norm was given a bar tab of $64,218 on the final episode of *Cheers*.

CHAPTER 4

LITERATURE

Do you know . . .

- How many lines are in a sonnet?
- Which famous and bestselling author also uses the pen name Robert Galbraith?
- To whom is *Moby-Dick* inscribed?
- Who became the first woman to receive the Pulitzer Prize for fiction?
- What is the title of the bestselling novel of the nineteenth century?

Do the answers to any of these questions jump into your mind? Are you dredging up all the info you learned in school? If not, the facts in this chapter are sure to jog your memory. The material here includes trivia for both classic and contemporary works, but it's always a good idea to bone up on the current bestseller lists anyway. There are several authors whose works are timeless—think Hemingway, Shakespeare, and Tolstoy—and questions about these authors and their works are sure to come up somewhat frequently at your trivia night.

BY THE NUMBERS
1 POINT

At **3,924** lines, *Hamlet* is Shakespeare's longest play. Agatha Christie took the title of her book *The Mousetrap* from the play, which is also the basis for *The Lion King*.

○°○°○○

Scheherazade is the narrator of the collection of stories called the ***One Thousand and One Nights***, or ***Arabian Nights***. Stories in this collection include "Aladdin's Wonderful Lamp," "Ali Baba and the Forty Thieves," and "The Seven Voyages of Sinbad the Sailor."

○°○°○○

Keep the following info in mind to improve your sense of literary time and appreciation of poetry.

- Sonnet—**fourteen lines**, usually iambic pentameter
- Fortnight—**fourteen days**
- Limerick—**five lines**
- Haiku—**three lines:** five syllables, seven syllables, five syllables
- Four score and seven years—**eighty-seven years**

○°○°○○

James Patterson and Maxine Paetro wrote **11th Hour**, which is the Women's Murder Club book eleven.

○[○]○[○]○

Truman Capote's best friend and neighbor, Harper Lee, wrote only **one** novel, *To Kill a Mockingbird*. It won the Pulitzer Prize for Fiction in 1961.

○[○]○[○]○

At the start of J.R.R. Tolkien's *The Lord of the Rings*, Bilbo Baggins celebrates his "**eleventy-first**" (111th) birthday.

○[○]○[○]○

In 1960, Dr. Seuss took a $50 bet with his editor, who said that Seuss could not write a book using only the same **fifty words**. Seuss won the bet with *Green Eggs and Ham*.

○[○]○[○]○

Ironically, the 1953 science fiction book ***Fahrenheit 451*** began appearing in a censored version in 1967. The title comes from the temperature at which paper catches fire.

○[○]○[○]○

William Shakespeare addressed **twenty-six** of his sonnets to a married woman known as the "Dark Lady" and **126** to a young man known as the "Fair Lord."

○[○]○[○]○

Uncle Tom's Cabin, by Harriet Beecher Stowe, was first published in 1852 and became the bestselling novel of the **nineteenth century** and the second bestselling book of the century after the Bible.

∘O∘O∘

The Hunt for Red October is Tom Clancy's **first** novel.

∘O∘O∘

Encyclopedia Brown is the protagonist of a series of successful books written by Donald J. Sobol, the **twenty-fourth** of which was published in 2007.

AUTHORS
3 POINTS

Ian Fleming introduced James Bond in his novel *Casino Royale*. Fleming, who also wrote *Chitty Chitty Bang Bang*, got the name for 007 from the author of a coffee table book on birds.

∘O∘O∘

Charles Dickens wrote classics such as *The Adventures of Oliver Twist*, *A Christmas Carol*, *David Copperfield*, *A Tale of Two Cities*, *Great Expectations*, and the unfinished work, *The Mystery of Edwin Drood*. The only life-size bronze statue of Dickens is located in Philadelphia. He decreed that no memorial was to be erected to honor him.

∘O∘O∘

Mark Twain was born Samuel Langhorne Clemens. He wrote *The Adventures of Tom Sawyer* (1876), the first typewritten book manuscript, and *Adventures of Huckleberry Finn*, which is set in the town where Twain grew up, Hannibal, Missouri. Twain was born when Halley's Comet passed Earth in 1835 and died of a heart attack on April 21, 1910, in Connecticut, one day after the comet's closest approach to Earth. Twain predicted this, and it came to pass.

 ₒ°ₒ°Oₒ

J.K. Rowling, who wrote the first Harry Potter novel in several cafes in Edinburgh, Scotland, uses the name Joanne Murray when conducting personal business. She has also secretly used the pen name Robert Galbraith to write crime novels, but her identity was revealed in 2013.

 ₒ°ₒ°Oₒ

Washington Irving wrote "The Legend of Sleepy Hollow" and "Rip Van Winkle," both set in the Catskills.

 ₒ°ₒ°Oₒ

Anne Rice was born Howard Allen Frances O'Brien in 1941. Rice, who was born Roman Catholic, became an atheist while writing *The Vampire Chronicles* and *Exit to Eden*.

 ₒ°ₒ°Oₒ

William Shakespeare is the bestselling author of all time, just ahead of Agatha Christie.

 ₒ°ₒ°Oₒ

Ernest Hemingway wrote that "a man must plant a tree, fight a bull, write a book, and have a son to prove his manhood." Hemingway published seven novels, winning the Nobel Prize for Literature in 1953 for *The Old Man and the Sea*. Hemingway traveled in Africa and lived in Europe; Key West, Florida; Cuba; and ultimately Ketchum, Idaho, where he shot himself in the head, which is the same way his father committed suicide.

○°○°○°○○

Edgar Allan Poe is credited with writing the first detective story, "The Murders in the Rue Morgue."

○°○°○°○○

Alexander Pushkin is considered the founder of modern Russian literature. Pushkin wrote *Eugene Onegin* and *The Queen of Spades*, both of which were turned into operas by Tchaikovsky.

○°○°○°○○

Roald Dahl wrote *James and the Giant Peach*, *Charlie and the Chocolate Factory*, *Fantastic Mr. Fox*, and the screenplays for Ian Fleming's novels *Chitty Chitty Bang Bang* and *You Only Live Twice*.

○°○°○°○○

English poet **Lord Byron** hosted a ghost story writing competition at a house he rented in Geneva, Switzerland. Mary Shelley was game and created *Frankenstein*.

○°○°○°○○

Herman Melville dedicated *Moby-Dick* to Nathaniel Hawthorne, to whom the book is inscribed.

AUTOBIOGRAPHIES

People love to talk about themselves, and they love to write about themselves too, some with a better sense of humor than others. Gain a sense of appreciation for the self-absorption of others and hone your trivia skills with these autobiographies.

- *Diary of a Genius*: Salvador Dali
- *Where's the Rest of Me?*: Ronald Reagan
- *Songs My Mother Taught Me*: Marlon Brando
- *The Hardest (Working) Man in Showbiz*: Ron Jeremy
- *sTORI Telling*: Tori Spelling
- *Here's the Deal: Don't Touch Me*: Howie Mandel
- *They Made a Monkee Out of Me*: Davy Jones
- *You Cannot Be Serious*: John McEnroe
- *Leading with My Chin*: Jay Leno
- *Don't Hassle the Hoff*: David Hasselhoff
- *Losing My Virginity*: Richard Branson
- *Out of Sync*: Lance Bass
- *Brainiac*: Ken Jennings
- *I Am Not Spock*: Leonard Nimoy
- *My Horizontal Life*: Chelsea Handler

PULITZER AND NOBEL PRIZES

5 POINTS

Pulitzer Prizes are endowed by **Columbia University**. An image of Benjamin Franklin is engraved on the gold medal that recipients are awarded.

。°○°○。

The Good Earth author, **Pearl S. Buck**, was the first woman to win both a Pulitzer Prize for Fiction and a Nobel Prize for Literature.

。°○°○。

Sinclair Lewis was awarded the Pulitzer in 1926 for his book *Arrowsmith*, but he declined the prize.

。°○°○。

In 1998, **Jose Saramago** became the first Portuguese-language writer to win a Nobel Prize for Literature.

。°○°○。

Roger Ebert is the only person to ever win a Pulitzer Prize for film commentary.

。°○°○。

Gone with the Wind, by Margaret Mitchell, and **All the King's Men**, by Robert Penn Warren, are the only two Pulitzer-winning novels to become Academy Award Best Picture–winning films.

∘°ₒ°O∘

Annie Proulx won the Pulitzer Prize for Fiction for *The Shipping News* (1996) and wrote a short story published in the *New Yorker* that inspired the screenplay for the movie *Brokeback Mountain* (2005).

∘°ₒ°O∘

Edith Wharton became the first woman to receive the Pulitzer Prize for Fiction with *The Age of Innocence* in 1921.

∘°ₒ°O∘

Doonesbury, created by Garry Trudeau, became the first daily comic strip to win a Pulitzer Prize for Best Editorial Cartoon in 1975. Trudeau is married to TV personality Jane Pauley.

∘°ₒ°O∘

Arthur Miller won a Pulitzer Prize for Drama for *Death of a Salesman* (1949).

∘°ₒ°O∘

Eugene O'Neill won four Pulitzer prizes, and he was the first American playwright awarded the Nobel Prize for Literature in 1936.

John F. Kennedy won the Pulitzer Prize for Biography for *Profiles in Courage* (1957). The book describes acts of bravery by eight U.S. Senators.

Andrew Jackson, the seventh U.S. president, is the subject of the Pulitzer Prize–winning book *American Lion*.

Jean-Paul Sartre declined the 1964 Nobel Prize for Literature. Boris Pasternak, author of *Doctor Zhivago*, refused the same award in 1958 under pressure from the Communist Party of the Soviet Union.

Four Irishmen have won the **Nobel Prize for Literature**: William Butler Yeats, George Bernard Shaw, Samuel Beckett, and Seamus Heaney.

In 1907 at the age of forty-two, **Rudyard Kipling**, born in India, became the youngest recipient of the Nobel Prize for Literature. He was also the first English-language writer to win the award.

Toni Morrison won the Pulitzer Prize for Fiction in 1988 for *Beloved* and the Nobel Prize for Literature in 1993.

BOOKS TURNED FLICKS
7 POINTS

A Time to Kill, John Grisham's first novel, was published in 1988, although it wasn't made into a movie until 1996.

∘°∘°∘∘

Jane Austin's book *Emma* was the inspiration for the Alicia Silverstone movie *Clueless* (1995).

∘°∘°∘∘

James Dickey wrote *Deliverance* (1970), and makes a cameo in the film (1972).

∘°∘°∘∘

Carl Sagan wrote the book *Contact* (1997), which inspired the Jodie Foster film.

∘°∘°∘∘

Irvine Welsh, author of *Trainspotting* (1996 film), plays a drug dealer in the film.

∘°∘°∘∘

Even Cowgirls Get the Blues, starring Uma Thurman, is based on a Tom Robbins book.

Blade Runner is based on Philip K. Dick's novel *Do Androids Dream of Electric Sheep?*.

∘°ₒ°O∘

William Shakespeare's **Twelfth Night** inspired *She's the Man* (2006) and is referenced several times in *Shakespeare in Love* (1998).

∘°ₒ°O∘

Roxanne (1987) is based on Edmond Rostand's **Cyrano de Bergerac**. Steve Martin's character C.D. Bales has the same initials.

∘°ₒ°O∘

Aaron Sorkin began writing the screenplay for **The Social Network** while author Ben Mezrich was still working on the manuscript to *The Accidental Billionaires*.

∘°ₒ°O∘

In 1959, the book **Starship Troopers** (1997 film) by Robert A. Heinlein was the first science fiction novel to be on the reading list of three of the five U.S. military branches.

TERMS INVENTED BY FAMOUS AUTHORS

 Birthday cards, public speeches, at work in the morning before you've had your coffee: it's sometimes hard to think of the right word, which is why these famous authors just made up their own. Keep these terms in mind for use at your next pub quiz. Or just make one up. Maybe it'll catch on . . .

- Chortle: Lewis Carroll
- Generation X: Douglas Coupland
- Big Brother: George Orwell
- Serendipity: Horace Walpole
- Yahoo: Jonathan Swift
- Nerd: Dr. Seuss
- Bump: William Shakespeare
- Tween: J.R.R. Tolkien
- Quark: James Joyce
- Utopia: Sir Thomas More

CHAPTER 5

MEDIA

Do you know . . .

- What U.S. newspaper has the highest daily circulation?
- Which popular website is named after a Hawaiian word?
- Who is the youngest model to grace the cover of *Cosmopolitan*?
- Who has appeared on the most covers of *Sports Illustrated*?
- What is the most widely syndicated cartoon panel in the world?

If you're not sure of the answers, it's time to brush up on your knowledge of all things media! The facts found in this chapter will give you a foot up on the competition, but to become unbeatable you will want to make sure that you're up-to-date on your current events before heading to a trivia night. Magazines, newspapers, and websites make for great trivia fodder, so be ready!

NEWSPAPERS
1 POINT

The **Hartford Courant** is America's oldest continuously published newspaper, established in 1764.

∘°∘°∘∘

The **New York Times** was founded in 1851 and has been continuously published in New York City ever since. It has won 112 Pulitzer Prizes, more than any other news organization.

∘°∘°∘∘

The **Wall Street Journal** has the highest daily circulation in the United States, followed by the *New York Times*, *USA Today*, and *Los Angeles Times*.

∘°∘°∘∘

The political newspaper associated with the Communist Party of the Soviet Union was called **Pravda**. When translated from Russian into English it means "truth." It ran from 1918 to 1991.

∘°∘°∘∘

Four of the top five newspapers with the largest circulation numbers in the world are based in **Japan**.

∘°∘°∘∘

In 1948, the **Chicago Daily Tribune** mistakenly ran the infamous headline "Dewey Defeats Truman."

∘O∘O∘

The Oakland Raiders were originally called the Señors, selected in a 1960 "Name the Team Contest" conducted by the **Oakland Tribune**. The name was changed to the third place selection after nine days.

∘O∘O∘

Debuting in 1960, **The Family Circus** is the most widely syndicated cartoon panel in the world, appearing in 1,500 newspapers.

∘O∘O∘

Garry Trudeau's **Doonesbury** cartoon first ran in the *Yale Daily News* in 1968.

∘O∘O∘

In March 2009 in Seattle, the **Post Intelligencer** became the first newspaper to go completely online.

ELECTRONIC MEDIA

3 POINTS

At its peak, **AOL** had thirty million subscribers worldwide, but this number was down to ten million in 2007 and continued to dwindle. In 2011, AOL purchased the *Huffington Post* to help boost their bottom line.

∘°∘°O∘

The ***Huffington Post*** was founded in 2005 by Arianna Huffington as a liberal outlet. In 2012, it became the first U.S. digital media company to win a Pulitzer Prize.

∘°∘°O∘

Wikipedia gets its name from the Hawaiian word for "fast."

∘°∘°O∘

Google, which was founded by Larry Page and Sergey Brin while they were students at Stanford University, registered its domain in 1997. The name comes from a misspelling of "googol," which is the number "one" followed by one hundred zeros.

∘°∘°O∘

Yahoo! was started in 1994 by David Filo and Jerry Yang, who in 1998 became the world's youngest billionaire at age twenty-nine.

TIME PERSON OF THE YEAR

 Every year, *Time* readers wait with bated breath to see who will take home the magazine's top honor. Good, bad, or ugly, the magazine shines a spotlight on their choice for the year's most important individual. Brush up on their choices to keep your team's trivia points in the black.

- 1927: Charles Lindbergh
- 1932, 1934, 1941: Franklin D. Roosevelt
- 1938: Adolf Hitler
- 1952: Elizabeth I
- 1963: Martin Luther King Jr.
- 1975: American Women
- 1994: Pope John Paul II
- 2006: You
- 2008, 2012: Barack Obama
- 2010: Mark Zuckerberg

Gawker, a media company and blog network, was started in Budapest, Hungary, in 2003.

∘°o°O∘

Twitter was started in 2006 by Jack Dorsey, who in 2008 was named as an outstanding innovator under the age of thirty-five by *MIT Technology Review*. In 2012, the *Wall Street Journal* named him the "Innovator of the Year" for technology.

∘°o°O∘

Craig Newmark started **Craigslist** in San Francisco in 1995. Angie Hicks started **Angie's List** in 1995 in Columbus, Ohio.

。°ₒ°O。

Entertainment media site *TMZ* is named for a thirty-mile section of Los Angeles that is centered at the intersection of West Beverly Boulevard and North La Cienega Boulevard, which is referred to as the "Thirty Mile Zone."

。°ₒ°O。

WordPress is the most popular blogging network on the web, with sixty million websites.

═══ ON THE COVER ═══
5 POINTS

Madonna has appeared on the cover of *Vanity Fair* more than any other person.

。°ₒ°O。

In 1974, *TV Guide* became the first magazine to sell one billion copies in a single year. Lucille Ball appeared on the first cover and holds the record for most cover features.

。°ₒ°O。

Charlie Chaplin was the first actor to appear on the cover of *Time* on July 6, 1925.

。°o°O°。

John Lennon was featured on the cover of the very first issue of ***Rolling Stone*** in 1967 wearing an army helmet. Run-D.M.C. was the first rap group to appear on the cover.

。°o°O°。

Tom Cruise was featured on the cover of ***GQ*** seven times between December 1988 and May 2006—more than any other person.

。°o°O°。

In 1975, Bruce Springsteen became the first musician to appear on the covers of *Time* and *Newsweek* in the same week, with the release of his album *Born to Run*.

。°o°O°。

In 1954, Roger Bannister appeared on the cover of ***Sports Illustrated*** for its first "Sportsman of the Year" issue. Bannister earned the cover for being the first person to run a mile in less than four minutes.

。°o°O°。

In May 1937, Jean Harlow became the first female actress to appear on the cover of ***Life***. She died the following month from influenza at the age of twenty-six.

○ °○° O ○

John Travolta became the first male to grace the cover of **McCall's** in 1978.

○ °○° O ○

k.d. lang appeared on the first cover of **Entertainment Weekly** on February 16, 1990.

○ °○° O ○

In 2012, Kesha appeared on the cover of **Vibe**, making her the first white female to appear on the cover by herself.

○ °○° O ○

Mia Farrow appeared on the cover of the first issue of **People** magazine on March 4, 1974.

○ °○° O ○

Oprah Winfrey has only ever shared the cover of **O, The Oprah Magazine** with two other women: First Lady Michelle Obama and fellow daytime host Ellen DeGeneres.

○ °○° O ○

Michael Jordan has appeared on the most covers of **Sports Illustrated**.

YOU SEXY THING

7 POINTS

Hugh Hefner founded *Playboy* in 1953. Marilyn Monroe was the first centerfold and Pamela Anderson appeared on the most covers with twelve.

o°o°O o

Penthouse was first published by **Bob Guccione** in 1969. His son Bob Guccione Jr. started *Spin* in 1985, and Madonna appeared on the first cover.

o°o°O o

Boston Strangler and O.J. Simpson attorney, **F. Lee Bailey** was also the publisher of the skin magazine *Gallery* in 1972.

o°o°O o

Burt Reynolds appeared as a nude centerfold for *Cosmopolitan* in 1972. Mario Lopez re-created the pose for *People* in 2008.

o°o°O o

At the age of fifteen in 1980, **Brooke Shields** became the youngest model ever to grace the cover of *Cosmopolitan*.

o°o°O o

Kim Basinger and **Charlize Theron** are the only two actresses to win an Oscar after appearing nude in *Playboy*.

○°○°○ ○

In 1976, **Jimmy Carter** became the first presidential hopeful to be the subject of a *Playboy* interview.

○°○°○ ○

Tyra Banks was the first African American woman to grace the covers of *GQ* and the *Sports Illustrated Swimsuit Issue*.

○°○°○ ○

In 1989, **Kathy Ireland** appeared on the cover of the twenty-fifth anniversary *Sports Illustrated Swimsuit Issue*, which was its bestselling edition of all time.

○°○°○ ○

In 2007, **Beyoncé Knowles** became the first nonmodel/nonathlete to grace the cover of the *Sports Illustrated Swimsuit Issue*. She is also the second African American woman to be featured on its cover.

○°○°○ ○

Jessica Biel posed topless in *Gear* magazine in hopes of being released from her contract on the TV series *Seventh Heaven*.

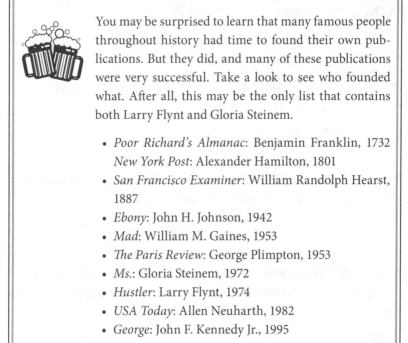

You may be surprised to learn that many famous people throughout history had time to found their own publications. But they did, and many of these publications were very successful. Take a look to see who founded what. After all, this may be the only list that contains both Larry Flynt and Gloria Steinem.

- *Poor Richard's Almanac*: Benjamin Franklin, 1732
  New York Post: Alexander Hamilton, 1801
- *San Francisco Examiner*: William Randolph Hearst, 1887
- *Ebony*: John H. Johnson, 1942
- *Mad*: William M. Gaines, 1953
- *The Paris Review*: George Plimpton, 1953
- *Ms.*: Gloria Steinem, 1972
- *Hustler*: Larry Flynt, 1974
- *USA Today*: Allen Neuharth, 1982
- *George*: John F. Kennedy Jr., 1995

Since 2004, *Esquire* has included an annual "Sexiest Woman Alive," and to date, **Scarlett Johansson** has nabbed the top honor twice.

∘°ₒ°O∘

Jenny McCarthy is the only "Playmate of the Year" to also appear on the cover of *Rolling Stone*.

∘°ₒ°O∘

Mel Gibson was *People*'s first "Sexiest Man Alive" in 1985. Sean Connery was the oldest at age fifty-nine. Richard Gere, Brad Pitt, George Clooney, and Johnny Depp have all received the honor twice.

ARTS AND SCIENCES

ROUND 2

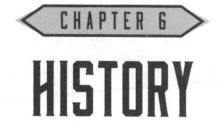

CHAPTER 6

HISTORY

Do you know . . .

- What country has the oldest constitution in the world?
- Who was president of the Confederacy?
- Which candy bar is named for a president's daughter?
- Which country suffered the greatest number of casualties during WWII?
- Who is the youngest First Lady in American history?

If you don't know the answers, don't feel too bad. History is a gigantic category, encompassing pretty much everything for all of time. That said, there are a few subjects that always pop up in trivia games—like the Civil War, the World Wars, etc.—so you should try to know as much about these topics as you can. While you're at it, memorize the names of the U.S. presidents and you'll have the leg up on the competition.

GENERAL HISTORY

1 POINT

Joan of Arc led the French army to victory at Orleans, a turning point in the Hundred Years' War. At age nineteen, she was turned over to the English and burned at the stake. Her remains were thrown into the Seine river on May 30, 1431.

∘°₀°○∘

English explorer **Sir Walter Raleigh** "discovered" and named Virginia, and introduced potatoes to Ireland. Raleigh was beheaded at the order of King James at the Palace of Whitehall, London, on October 29, 1618, after Spanish outposts were sacked in Venezuela during Raleigh's search of El Dorado, the "Lost City of Gold."

∘°₀°○∘

In 1620, after one failed attempt, the **Mayflower** finally departed on its journey to America from the English port, Plymouth. Another ship, the *Speedwell*, was supposed to accompany the *Mayflower* but was leaking too badly to make the voyage.

∘°₀°○∘

San Marino (1600), the United States (1789), Norway (1814), and Belgium (1831) have the four oldest **constitutions** in the world.

∘°₀°○∘

Switzerland, known for its neutrality, has not been to war with another country since 1515.

₀°ₒ°O₀

Sri Lanka, formerly known as Ceylon, was the first nation to have a female prime minister. Sirimavo Bandaranaike, the widow of late Prime Minister S.W.R.D. Bandaranaike, took office in 1960.

₀°ₒ°O₀

Suffragette **Susan B. Anthony** famously said that the bicycle had "done more to emancipate women than anything else in the world."

₀°ₒ°O₀

Iowa and **Mississippi** are the only two states that have never elected a female governor, senator, or member of the House.

₀°ₒ°O₀

In 1989, **South Africa** became the only nation to have created nuclear weapons and then to have voluntarily disarmed itself.

₀°ₒ°O₀

One of history's largest refugee migrations took place between 1947 and 1951 when about fifteen million people traveled between **Pakistan** and **India**.

China was known to Europeans as **Cathay** from the eleventh century until the sixteenth century.

Damascus, the capital of Syria, is the oldest continuously inhabited city in the world. It ruled over Israel at the time of the Hanukkah story.

Heads of state from France, the United States, Italy, Spain, and Austria were all assassinated by **anarchists** between 1892 and 1901.

THE CIVIL WAR
3 POINTS

The first shots of the American Civil War were fired on April 12, 1861, when **Fort Sumter** in Charleston, South Carolina, was attacked. The war lasted one day short of four years and four weeks and claimed the lives of 600,000 soldiers.

Abner Doubleday, who is said to have invented baseball, fired the first shots in defense of Fort Sumter.

Jefferson Davis was the president of the Confederacy, which was made up of eleven southern states in favor of keeping slavery in the United States. Interestingly, Missouri and Kentucky are represented in the thirteen stars on the Confederate flag, though they never actually seceded from the Union.

On July 1, 1861, the **First Battle of Bull Run** in Manassas, Virginia, was the first major land battle fought. The majority of U.S. Civil War battles took place in Virginia.

The **Battle of Antietam** on September 17, 1862, was the bloodiest battle in a single day in American history. More than 22,000 were dead, wounded, or missing in the battle that took place near Sharpsburg, Maryland.

"**Copperhead**" was the name given to a Northern sympathizer living in the South.

General George Meade commanded the Union Army at the **Battle of Gettysburg**, which was fought from July 1st to 3rd, 1863. There were around 50,000 casualties.

President Abraham Lincoln was assassinated on April 15, 1865, just six days after General Robert E. Lee of the Confederacy formally surrendered to General Ulysses S. Grant of the Union at the Appomattox Court House in Virginia.

∘°ₒ°O∘

The last land battle of the **U.S. Civil War** was fought in Texas on May 12 and 13, 1865.

∘°ₒ°O∘

 In 1865, General Sherman issued **"Special Field Order No. 15,"** which offered slave families forty acres and a mule as reparations. In 1986, Spike Lee used this for the name of his production company: 40 Acres and a Mule Filmworks.

∘°ₒ°O∘

Union general Lewis Wallace wrote ***Ben-Hur: A Tale of the Christ*** (1880), which was later adapted into an Oscar-winning film.

∘°ₒ°O∘

Tennessee was the first Confederate state to be readmitted to the Union after the Civil War. Georgia was the last.

You probably know that the United States declared independence from England in 1776, but there are a lot of other countries whose independence came much later, and from countries you might not expect, including:

- Haiti from France: 1804
- Mexico from Spain: 1810
- Brazil from Portugal: 1822
- Cuba from the United States: 1902
- Finland from Russia: 1917
- Iceland from Denmark: 1918
- India from England: 1947
- Madagascar from France: 1960
- South Sudan from Sudan: 2011

PRESIDENTS
5 POINTS

Benjamin Harrison accidentally shuffled the admission orders for North and South Dakota, meaning that no one knows which was the thirty-ninth state and which was the fortieth.

○°○°○°

The most common **presidential birth states** are Virginia (8), Ohio (7), Massachusetts (4), and New York (4). North Carolina, Texas, and Vermont have 2 each.

Jimmy Carter was the first president born in a hospital.

Four presidents have won the Nobel Peace Prize: Theodore Roosevelt in 1906, Woodrow Wilson in 1919, Jimmy Carter in 2002, and Barack Obama in 2009.

Teddy Roosevelt, an avid hunter, killed 296 animals, including nine lions and eight elephants, in an eleven-month period. He was also the first sitting president to leave the United States, visiting Panama in 1906.

Having traveled to China in 1899 at age twenty-four, **Herbert Hoover** would speak Chinese with his wife when they didn't want to be understood by others. Martin Van Buren grew up speaking Dutch, and English was his second language.

John Adams and Thomas Jefferson died on the same day, **July 4, 1826**, on the fiftieth anniversary of the signing of the Declaration of Independence for the United States of America.

Abraham Lincoln was the first president born outside of the original thirteen colonies (he was born in Kentucky). **Andrew Jackson**, though primarily from Tennessee, was born somewhere along the border of the Carolinas.

$\circ \, {}^{\circ}O_{\circ}{}^{\circ} O \circ$

Abraham Lincoln and Lyndon B. Johnson were the tallest presidents at six foot four inches. **James Madison** was the shortest at five foot four inches.

$\circ \, {}^{\circ}O_{\circ}{}^{\circ} O \circ$

Charles Darwin and Abraham Lincoln were born on the same day, February 12, 1809.

$\circ \, {}^{\circ}O_{\circ}{}^{\circ} O \circ$

Ronald Reagan won a record 525 electoral votes. He was also the oldest elected president and the first divorced person to become president.

$\circ \, {}^{\circ}O_{\circ}{}^{\circ} O \circ$

On March 30, 1981, **John Hinckley Jr.** shot Ronald Reagan in the chest and lower arm, causing superficial injuries. Press Secretary James Brady, who was also shot, was paralyzed. Hinckley was found not guilty by reason of insanity and remains in a psychiatric facility in Washington, D.C.

$\circ \, {}^{\circ}O_{\circ}{}^{\circ} O \circ$

Teddy Roosevelt became the youngest president at age forty-two when he was sworn in after William McKinley's assassination. John F. Kennedy (JFK) was the youngest elected commander in chief at age forty-three.

○°○°O○

William Howard Taft and JFK are buried in Arlington National Cemetery.

○°○°O○

Lincoln, **McKinley**, and **Kennedy** were all shot on a Friday.

○°○°O○

Gerald Ford, born Leslie Lynch King Jr., is the only president who was never elected to vice president or president. He is also the only Eagle Scout to become president.

○°○°O○

Aaron Burr was the first U.S. vice president who did not go on to become president. Although Burr killed Secretary of the Treasury Alexander Hamilton in a duel in 1804, Hamilton seems to have won historically—he appears on the $10 bill.

○°○°O○

In 1868, **Andrew Johnson** became the first president to be impeached. Bill Clinton was also impeached in 1998.

∘°∘°∘

Dwight Eisenhower was the first president to govern all fifty U.S. states.

∘°∘°∘

Charles J. Guiteau assassinated **James Garfield** in 1881.

∘°∘°∘

William Henry Harrison delivered the longest inaugural address in history—8,444 words!—without a coat in the rain. Due to this lengthy speech, Harrison holds the record for shortest term in office. He died from pneumonia after just thirty days in office in 1841.

∘°∘°∘

Grover Cleveland, the only U.S. president to serve two nonconsecutive terms, married Frances Folsom at the White House in 1886. At twenty-two years old, she is the youngest First Lady in American history.

∘°∘°∘

Grover Cleveland's daughter Ruth inspired the name for the Baby Ruth candy bar.

∘°∘°∘

Andrew Jackson, the first president of Irish descent, killed Charles Dickinson in a duel in 1806. The man accused the future president of cheating on a horse race bet and also insulted Jackson's wife, Rachel.

WWII
7 POINTS

D-day was June 6, 1944. Troops from Britain, Canada, France, and the United States were commanded by General Dwight D. Eisenhower in the largest invasion fleet in history. The "D" in D-day stands for "day."

∘°ₒ°O∘

Mickey Mouse was the Allied soldiers' password on D-day. Higgins boats were used to transport soldiers to the code-named beaches of Utah, Omaha, Gold, Juno, and Sword.

∘°ₒ°O∘

American military used the **Navajo** language for coded communication. German military used the "Enigma" to encode strategic messages before and during World War II.

∘°ₒ°O∘

Operation Tannenbaum was the planned Nazi invasion of neutral Switzerland. Hitler described Switzerland as "a pimple on the face of Europe" but never gave the go-ahead for the invasion.

The **Battle of Stalingrad** (September 1942–January 1943) is one of the bloodiest battles in the history of warfare and is considered the turning point in WWII. The battle resulted in more than a million casualties.

○ ○°○°○ ○

The **Soviet Union** suffered more casualties—8.7 million—than any other nation during WWII.

○ ○°○°○ ○

Italy was the first Axis nation to surrender to the Allies. Italian leader **Benito Mussolini** was hung upside down in public.

○ ○°○°○ ○

Anne Frank hid in an attic in Amsterdam during WWII until she and her family were found. She was placed in a concentration camp where she died of typhus.

○ ○°○°○ ○

Glenn Miller, who recorded the first Gold record, died in a plane crash over the English Channel on December 15, 1944.

○ ○°○°○ ○

Catch-22 author **Joseph Heller** flew sixty combat missions as a bombardier with the U.S. Air Force in Europe during WWII.

₀ᵒₒᵒᴼₒ

John F. Kennedy commanded a PT-109 navy boat in the South Pacific.

₀ᵒₒᵒᴼₒ

The **Battle of the Bulge** was the last major German onslaught in World War II and took place from December 1944 through January 1945.

₀ᵒₒᵒᴼₒ

Veterans Day was known as Armistice Day until the end of WWII. Armistice Day commemorated the end of WWI.

In 1936, Edward VIII became King of the United Kingdom and the Dominions of the British Commonwealth, and Emperor of India (his business cards had to be printed in a very small font). The only problem was that he was in love with twice-divorced American socialite Wallis Simpson. The Church of England (of which Edward was the head) did not allow the remarriage of divorced people with living former spouses, and the idea of Simpson as Queen of England did not sit well either. So rather than create a constitutional crisis, Edward abdicated his throne to his brother (you may remember him from *The King's Speech*) King George VI, who is responsible for the current brood of royals, including Queen Elizabeth II, Prince Charles, Princes William and Harry, and, of course, the royal baby, Prince George.

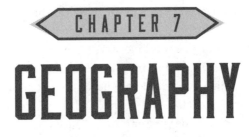

CHAPTER 7

GEOGRAPHY

Do you know . . .

- What is the only two-word state that has a two-word state capital?
- Where is the tallest mountain in the continental United States?
- What is the largest lake in New England?
- How long is the longest river in the world?
- What is the largest National Park in the continental United States?

Can't come up with all of the answers? Don't worry. The facts in this chapter are what you need to rock the geography section of your local pub quiz. Geography is a big topic, to be sure. But even though you are dealing with the entire world, the answer to any geography question is usually guessable, and there is a limited, minimally changing and expanding pool of information to work with. Mountains, bodies of water, and lines across the land have created cultures, countries, and continents—so keep those in mind. Also, make sure you know your state capitals! We'll review a few with interesting origins here.

STATE CAPITAL FACTS

1 POINT

South Dakota is the only state whose capital city, **Pierre**, does not share any of the same letters with the name of the state.

∘°∘°O∘

Bismarck, North Dakota, is the only U.S. state capital that ends in three consonants.

∘°∘°O∘

Phoenix lies on the Salt River. With more than one million residents, Phoenix has the largest population of any state capital. It's also the fourth most populous city in the United States.

∘°∘°O∘

Four state capitals are named for U.S. presidents: **Jackson**, Mississippi; **Jefferson City**, Missouri; **Lincoln**, Nebraska; and **Madison**, Wisconsin.

∘°∘°O∘

St. Paul, Minnesota, and **Baton Rouge**, Louisiana, are the two state capitals located on the Mississippi River.

∘°∘°O∘

Baton Rouge, which means "red stick," is named for a post that marked a boundary between Indian tribes. Des Moines (for "city of monks"), Iowa; Pierre, South Dakota; and Montpelier, Vermont, are the other state capitals that have French names.

○ °○° ○ ○

Montpelier has the smallest population of any state capital, and is the only state capital without a Mc-Donald's.

○ °○° ○ ○

Of the forty-eight continental states, **Olympia**, Washington, is the most northern and most western capital. Austin, Texas, holds the record for southernmost state capital.

○ °○° ○ ○

Carson City, Nevada, and **Trenton**, New Jersey, are the two state capitals that sit on the border of other states, California and Pennsylvania, respectively.

○ °○° ○ ○

The Republic of Texas (1836–1848), and now state of Texas, has moved its capital city twelve times. Its locations have included Galveston, Houston, and **Austin**, which is the current capital.

○ °○° ○ ○

Oklahoma City, Oklahoma, and **Indianapolis**, Indiana, are the two state capitals that contain the name of their state.

₀°₀°O₀

Two state capitals are named for royalty: **Annapolis**, Maryland, was named for Princess Anne of Denmark and Norway, who became Queen of Great Britain. **Albany**, New York, was named in honor of the Duke of York and Albany, who later became King James II of England and James VII of Scotland.

₀°₀°O₀

At 7,000 feet, **Santa Fe** is the state capital with the highest elevation. Settled in 1609, the New Mexico capital is the oldest capital city in North America. In addition, it is the only two-word state capital that belongs to a two-word state.

≡ MOUNTAINS ≡
3 POINTS

The Appalachian Trail runs 2,200 miles from Springer Mountain, Georgia, to Mount Katahdin, Maine. The highest point on the trail is **Mt. Mitchell** (6,684 feet) in North Carolina, which is also the highest mountain in the eastern United States. There is an unofficial International Appalachian Trail that ends in Newfoundland.

₀°₀°O₀

Mount Logan, near the Alaskan border, is the highest peak in Canada at 19,551 feet, and is the second tallest in North America after Mount McKinley/Denali, which stands at 20,237 feet.

∘°∘°O∘

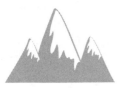 The tallest mountains in the Americas are in the Andes in South America, which, at 4,500 miles long, are also the longest mountain range in the world. The tallest peak in this range is **Mount Aconcagua** in Argentina (22,837 feet).

∘°∘°O∘

Mt. Kilimanjaro (19,341 feet) is the highest mountain in Africa. It gets its name from Swahili for "shining hill" for its glaciers, which are predicted to disappear by the year 2022.

∘°∘°O∘

Mount Mansfield (4,393) is the tallest mountain in Vermont. It is located in the town of Stowe, where the von Trapp family settled when they left Europe.

∘°∘°O∘

Located in the Cascade range, **Mt. Rainier** (14,411 feet) overlooks Seattle and is Washington's highest peak. It is considered one of the most dangerous volcanoes in the world.

∘°∘°O∘

The tallest mountain in the contiguous forty-eight states is **Mount Whitney** (14,505 feet) and is located in the Sierra Nevada range in California. The lowest point in the United States is Death Valley, California, which is also the largest National Park in the lower forty-eight states.

○°○°○○

The Apennine Mountains make up the spine of Italy. **Corno Grande** (Big Horn) is the highest peak (9,554 feet) in this range.

○°○°○○

Turkey's highest peak, **Mt. Ararat** (16,854 ft), is believed to be where Noah landed his ark.

○°○°○○

The highest peak of Antarctica, the continent with the highest average elevation (more than 6,500 feet), is **Vinson Massif** (16,050 feet).

○°○°○○

The second tallest mountain in the world is Pakistan's **K2** at 28,251 feet.

○°○°○○

Located in Sagarmatha National Park, **Mount Everest** (29,028) is the tallest in the world. New Zealander Sir Edmund Hillary and Sherpa Tenzing Norgay were the first to climb Everest and return safely in

1953. The four flags they left at the top were for Great Britain, Nepal, the United Nations, and India.

THE GREAT LAKES

The Great Lakes, which are located in the northeastern United States and southeastern Canada, are the largest group of freshwater lakes in the world. In order of size, they are Lake Superior, Lake Ontario, Lake Michigan, Lake Huron, and Lake Erie. In the United States, they border eight states: Minnesota, Wisconsin, Michigan, Illinois, Indiana, Ohio, Pennsylvania, and New York. In 1998, President Clinton signed a bill that briefly made Lake Champlain the sixth Great Lake, but a few weeks later the Senate voted to downgrade it to simply a good lake.

The remains of **George Mallory**, who famously climbed Mt. Everest "because it is there," were found on May 2, 1999, nearly seventy-five years after he disappeared on Mt. Everest. He may have been the first to climb it.

o°o°o°o

Bear Grylls of the television show *Man vs. Wild* is the youngest British person to summit Mt. Everest at twenty-three years old.

o°o°o°o

Mauna Kea is the world's tallest mountain when measured from its underwater base to the peak, 33,480 feet (13,796 feet above sea level).

The tallest mountain in the known universe is **Olympus Mons**, Mars, sixteen miles high (69,459 feet).

═══ RIVERS ═══
5 POINTS

The **Volga** is the longest river in Europe. It empties into the Caspian Sea.

Europe's second longest river, the **Danube**, flows into the Black Sea. Four countries have capital cities on the Danube: Serbia (Belgrade), Slovakia (Bratislava), Hungary (Budapest), and Austria (Vienna).

Opened to the public in 1843, the world's first underwater tunnel was constructed under the river Thames in London, England. While the Thames is impressive, the river **Severn** is the longest river in Great Britain.

Five of the world's ten longest rivers are in Asia. The **Amur River** (number ten on that list) makes up most of the border between China and Russia.

The **Murray River** is the longest in Australia and the fifteenth longest in the world.

∘°₀°O∘

Mesopotamia takes its name from the Greek for "between two rivers." These rivers are the **Tigris** and **Euphrates**.

∘°₀°O∘

The river **Amstel** divides the Dutch capital of Amsterdam in two.

∘°₀°O∘

At 3,976 miles, the **Amazon** is the second longest river in the world. (The Nile in Africa is the first at 4,132 miles.) The Amazon begins in Peru and gets its name from the Greek for "missing one breast." The Paraná is the second longest river in South America.

∘°₀°O∘

The **Río de la Plata**, the widest river in the world, separates Argentina and Uruguay.

∘°₀°O∘

The **River Shannon** is the longest river in Ireland.

∘°₀°O∘

The **Zambezi River** in Zambia and Zimbabwe forms Victoria Falls, the world's largest waterfall.

The **Ebola** virus is named for the river of its origin located in the Democratic Republic of the Congo. The virus first surfaced in 1977, killing hundreds, and it returned in 1995 to kill hundreds more.

The **Niagara River** connects Lake Erie to Lake Ontario.

Hernando de Soto was the first European to discover the **Mississippi River**, North America's largest. In 1542, while on its banks, de Soto died from a fever.

Pittsburgh's **Three Rivers Stadium** is named for the Allegheny, Monongahela, and Ohio Rivers. Pittsburgh has more bridges than any other American city.

The **Ohio River** forms the border between Kentucky and Indiana. The Connecticut River forms the border between Vermont and New Hampshire. The Columbia River forms 300 miles of the Oregon–Washington border.

The **Colorado River**, which ultimately flows into the Gulf of California/ Sea of Cortez, created the Grand Canyon. In 1540, Francisco Coronado was the first European to behold the Grand Canyon.

∘°ₒ°O∘

The **Snake River** on the Oregon–Idaho border runs through Hell's Canyon, the deepest gorge in the United States.

∘°ₒ°O∘

Iowa is the only state whose entire eastern and western borders are formed by rivers.

∘°ₒ°O∘

The **Klondike River** gave its name to the gold rush that took place in the Yukon territory, Canada, in 1896.

WHAT'S IN A NAME?
7 POINTS

The most densely populated U.S. state, **New Jersey**, is named for an island in the English Channel.

∘°ₒ°O∘

The **fez**, a brimless, red felt hat in the shape of a truncated cone, is named for the Moroccan city where it originates. The famous textile pattern **paisley** is named for a Scottish town near Glasgow.

○ °○° ○ ○

Lyme disease, first diagnosed in 1975, is named for the town in Connecticut where it was discovered.

○ °○° ○ ○

Cheddar, created at the beginning of the twelfth century, was first made in and named for a small village in Somerset, England. Wiener schnitzel is named for Vienna, or Wien, Austria.

○ °○° ○ ○

Denim is named for the city where it was first created, Nimes, France. Duffel, a traditional heavy wool fabric, is named for a city in Belgium.

○ °○° ○ ○

Pilsner (Pilzen) is named for the town where it was first brewed in the former Czechoslovakia.

○ °○° ○ ○

The **Canary Islands** are named for their wild dogs (Latin: *Canis*). The songbirds were named after the islands.

Lake Champlain, the largest lake in New England, separates New York and Vermont. This lake is named for the founder of the city of Quebec, Samuel de Champlain.

Dallas, Texas, is named for George Dallas, James Polk's vice president.

Alcatraz is named for the Spanish word for the "strange birds" or "pelicans" that once inhabited the island.

Brazil is named for a tree, brazilwood, or brazilleros. Its wood yields a red dye called "brazilin."

Barcelona is named for Hamilcar Barca, a Carthaginian general who is the father of Hannibal.

The **Cook Strait** separates the two large islands of New Zealand and is named for James Cook, who was the first to circumnavigate the islands.

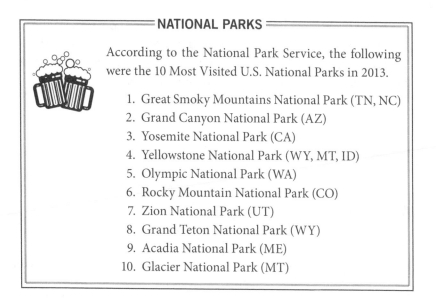

NATIONAL PARKS

According to the National Park Service, the following were the 10 Most Visited U.S. National Parks in 2013.

1. Great Smoky Mountains National Park (TN, NC)
2. Grand Canyon National Park (AZ)
3. Yosemite National Park (CA)
4. Yellowstone National Park (WY, MT, ID)
5. Olympic National Park (WA)
6. Rocky Mountain National Park (CO)
7. Zion National Park (UT)
8. Grand Teton National Park (WY)
9. Acadia National Park (ME)
10. Glacier National Park (MT)

The archipelago **Tierra del Fuego** (Spanish for "land of fire") was named by the Portuguese explorer Ferdinand Magellan, who was the first European there. The many fires of the Yaghan people were visible from what would become the Magellan Strait, inspiring the name.

∘°○°○∘

In 1488, Bartholomeu Dias named the Cape of Storms (what is now the **Cape of Good Hope**). The Cape of Good Hope—as named by King John II—was once thought to be the southern tip of Africa, but technically this title is held by Cape Agulhas, which lies ninety miles to the southeast.

∘°○°○∘

The name of **Portland, Oregon**, was decided by a coin toss in 1845. Founders Francis Pettygrove of Portland, Maine, and Asa Lovejoy from Boston, Massachusetts, went for the best two out of three in the coin toss to name the city. Victory for Pettygrove. Victory Portland.

CHAPTER 8

ART

Do you know . . .

- What is the most visited museum in the world?
- What is Rembrandt's last name?
- Who designed the uniforms of the Swiss Guard?
- Which American painter is called the "Painter of Light"?
- Which artist created the bronze cast for "The Thinker"?

If you're not sure how to answer these questions, don't worry about it. Art is a wildcard category and it doesn't come up that frequently. But knowing a few key facts in this category can put your team over the edge in a tight trivia game. Most people don't have a very extensive art history background, but if you know a major painting or two from big artists (think Picasso, van Gogh, Michelangelo, etc.), then you should be fine. To make sure you're really ready to impress your teammates— and your opponents—you should also brush up on various famous museums and even familiarize yourself with the art used for some well-known album covers. Sound good? Then get ready to get your art on.

MUSEUMS
1 POINT

The **Van Gogh Museum** in Amsterdam is the most visited museum in the Netherlands, though Vincent van Gogh sold only one painting while he was alive, titled *Red Vineyard at Arles*.

∘°ₒ°O∘

Frank Lloyd Wright designed the **Guggenheim Museum** in Manhattan, which was completed in 1959, the same year the architect died. It's known as "The Museum of Non-Objective Painting."

∘°ₒ°O∘

Established in 1954, the **J. Paul Getty Museum** was commissioned by billionaire Jean Paul Getty, who founded Getty Oil. The museum is one of the most visited in the United States, with more than a million visitors annually.

∘°ₒ°O∘

The **Norman Rockwell Museum** is located in Stockbridge, Massachusetts, where Rockwell (1894–1978) moved in 1953. In 2013, Rockwell's painting *Saying Grace* became the most expensive American painting ever sold at auction when it went for $46 million at Sotheby's in New York City.

∘°ₒ°O∘

Some **lesser-known museums** that celebrate a potpourri of subjects include the following:

- Spam Museum—Austin, Minnesota
- Dr Pepper Museum—Waco, Texas
- Nobel Museum—Stockholm, Sweden
- World of Coca-Cola—Atlanta, Georgia
- The Hershey Story, The Museum of Chocolate Avenue—Hershey, Pennsylvania
- American Jazz Museum and Negro Leagues Baseball Museum—Kansas City, Missouri
- National Atomic Testing Museum and the Burlesque Hall of Fame—Las Vegas, Nevada

∘°ₒ°O∘

The **Smithsonian Institution** was established in 1846 by decree of British scientist James Smithson's will. It is the world's largest museum complex with nineteen museums and more than 140 million items, including the Hope Diamond, Dorothy's ruby slippers from *The Wizard of Oz*, a Concorde airplane, and Archie Bunker's chair.

∘°ₒ°O∘

In 1990, the biggest property theft in history occurred at the **Isabella Stewart Gardner Museum** in Boston. Thieves dressed as Boston police officers stole $500 million worth of art. Works by Johannes Vermeer, Rembrandt van Rijn, Édouard Manet, Edgar Degas, and Govaert Flinck were cut from frames on the wall. By a request in Gardner's will, the frames remain empty on the walls and cannot be replaced.

∘°ₒ°O∘

Madame Marie Tussaud created her first wax figure in 1777, of Voltaire. In 1835, she opened her first wax museum on Baker Street, London. Madame Tussaud now has a dozen wax museum locations across the globe.

∘°ₒ°O∘

Salvador Dali is buried in a crypt under a glass dome in the **Dalí Theatre and Museum** in his hometown of Figueres, in the Catalonia region of Spain. The largest collection of his works, outside of Europe, is located at the Dali Museum in St. Petersburg, Florida.

∘°ₒ°O∘

Madrid is home to the **Museo del Prado**, which was founded in 1819. The museum features an extensive collection of works by Francisco de Goya, but *Las Meninas* by Velázquez is the best-known work on display.

∘°ₒ°O∘

With more than nine million visitors each year, the **Louvre** in Paris is the most visited museum in the world, in the most visited country in the world, France. Its most famous work is Leonardo da Vinci's *Mona Lisa*.

∘°ₒ°O∘

The Field Museum in Chicago is a natural history museum that features Sue, the world's largest Tyrannosaurus rex skeleton.

∘°ₒ°O∘

Founded in 1812, the oldest natural history museum in the United States—the **Academy of Natural Sciences of Drexel University**—is located in Philadelphia, which is also home to America's first zoo.

$_\circ {}^{\circ} {}_\circ {}^{\circ} \bigcirc \circ$

The **Metropolitan Museum of Art** (the Met) in New York City is the largest art museum in the United States. In 1961, the Met purchased Rembrandt's painting *Aristotle Contemplating a Bust of Homer* for $2.3 million.

═══ PAINTERS ═══
3 POINTS

Raphael, an Italian High Renaissance artist, was born on Good Friday in 1483 and died on Good Friday in 1520. Many of his biblical depictions can be found in Vatican Palace, having been painted for two Popes.

$_\circ {}^{\circ} {}_\circ {}^{\circ} \bigcirc \circ$

Alessandro di Mariano Filipepi, whose nickname **Botticelli** means "little barrel," was born in 1445 in Italy. Botticelli's better-known works include *Primavera* (1482) and *Birth of Venus* (1486).

$_\circ {}^{\circ} {}_\circ {}^{\circ} \bigcirc \circ$

Michelangelo (1475–1564) designed the uniforms of the Swiss Guard and sculpted tombs for Giuliano and Lorenzo, members of the

Florence, Italy, Medici family. Pope Julius II commissioned Michelangelo to paint the Sistine Chapel ceiling in the sixteenth century.

∘°ₒ°O∘

El Greco (The Greek) was born in 1541 and is considered the greatest and most individualistic Spanish painter, known for his color contrast and elongated figures.

∘°ₒ°O∘

Rembrandt van Rijn (1606–1669) was a Dutch painter who is known for his self-portraits, portraits of his contemporaries, and biblical depictions.

∘°ₒ°O∘

Vincent van Gogh, who was very fond of absinthe, cut off a piece of his ear in 1888. The artist committed suicide at age thirty-seven in 1890 while painting *Wheat Field with Crows*.

∘°ₒ°O∘

Paul Gauguin is a French painter who is famous for his scenes of Tahiti, where he spent many years of his life, fathering several children with a mistress native to the island. A Post-Impressionist artist, Gauguin did not receive much recognition until after his death, at the age of fifty-four, in 1903.

○°ₒ°○°

Pablo Picasso was a Spanish painter and sculptor who spent most of his adult life in France. Picasso is the only living artist to have had his work displayed in the Grand Gallery of the Louvre. His famous painting *Guernica* depicts atrocities during the Spanish Civil War. Picasso, who lived to be ninety-one years old, died in 1973.

○°ₒ°○°

Claude Monet (1840–1926) is famed for his paintings of the water lilies in his garden. He is considered to be one of the first Impressionist painters. Édouard Manet was his good friend.

○°ₒ°○°

Édouard Manet (1832–1883) played a pivotal role in the transition from Realism to Impressionism. *The Luncheon on the Grass* (*Le déjeuner sur l'herbe*) and *Olympia* (both 1863) inspired young painters to create art using Impressionist techniques.

○°ₒ°○°

Edgar Degas (1834–1917) was a French painter and sculptor best known for his racing and ballet pictures created during the nineteenth century Impressionism art movement. His *Dancers* painting fetched $11 million at auction in 1997.

○°ₒ°○°

Winslow Homer was born in Boston in 1836 but spent his last twenty-seven years in Prouts Neck, Maine. Stamps issued by the U.S.

Postal Service in 1962 and 2012 commemorated his paintings *Breezing Up* and *Boys in a Pasture* respectively.

∘°ₒ°O∘

Vanessa Bell (1879–1961) was an English painter and interior designer. Her sister was the author Virginia Woolf. Bell is portrayed by Miranda Richardson in the film *The Hours* (2002); Nicole Kidman played Woolf.

∘°ₒ°O∘

Salvador Dali (1902–1989) was a Surrealist painter who used the pseudonym Avida Dollars, meaning "Eager for Dollars." His eccentric behavior often drew more attention than his art.

∘°ₒ°O∘

American painter **LeRoy Neiman** is most famous for his paintings of athletes.

∘°ₒ°O∘

Jackson Pollock's painting *No. 5, 1948* became the second most expensive painting sold at auction when David Geffen sold it in 2006 for $140 million. Pollock died at the age of forty-four in a drunk-driving accident on August 11, 1956.

∘°ₒ°O∘

Sacramento born **Thomas Kinkade**, "Painter of Light," called himself "America's most collected living artist" before his death in 2012 at the age of fifty-eight. It's estimated that one in twenty American homes has a copy of one of his paintings.

∘ °₀°O ∘

Andy Warhol (born in 1928) grew up in Pittsburgh, where a museum is exclusively dedicated to his work. Warhol, known for pop art, famously coined the term "fifteen minutes of fame." The highest price ever paid for a work by Andy Warhol was $100 million for *Eight Elvises* (1963).

MOST FAMOUS WORKS

Not an art history major? If you need a quick reference for which famous works belong to which artist, look no further. There's a good chance that one of these facts will come up at one of your quiz nights, so brush up before you head in.

- Edvard Munch: *The Scream*
- Pablo Picasso: *Guernica*
- Johannes Vermeer: *Girl with a Pearl Earring*
- Vincent van Gogh: *Starry Night*
- Sandro Botticelli: *Birth of Venus*
- Claude Monet: *Water Lilies*
- Rembrandt van Rijn: *The Night Watch*
- Michelangelo: *The Creation of Adam* (The Sistine Chapel)
- Leonardo da Vinci: *Mona Lisa*
- Salvador Dali: *The Persistence of Memory*

≡ SCULPTORS ≡

5 POINTS

Donatello was a Florentine sculptor who created the bronze statue of *David* (1432), which was eclipsed by Michelangelo's *David* a century later.

∘°ₒ°O∘

Venus de Milo, a statue depicting the Greek goddess Aphrodite, was found on the Greek island of Melos in 1820.

∘°ₒ°O∘

Michelangelo created the sculpture *Pietà*, which depicts the Virgin Mary holding her son, Jesus Christ. The marble slab, which is the only work by Michelangelo that bears his signature, is located at St. Peter's Basilica in Vatican City.

∘°ₒ°O∘

Gian Lorenzo Bernini (1598–1680) created *Rape of Proserpina* (1622), *David* (1624), and *Apollo and Daphne* (1625).

∘°ₒ°O∘

Constantin Brancusi (1876–1957) created *The Kiss* (1908) and the outdoor sculpture *The Endless Column* (1938).

∘°ₒ°O∘

Auguste Rodin created the bronze cast *The Thinker* and the *Gates of Hell*, both inspired by Dante's *Divine Comedy* (1321).

∘°ₒ°○∘

Robert Indiana created *LOVE* in 1964. The design was made into a postage stamp in 1973, and inspired many sculptures.

∘°ₒ°○∘

Easter Island, Chile, contains hundreds of stone monoliths that stand, on average, thirteen feet high and weigh fourteen tons.

∘°ₒ°○∘

Crazy Horse is the subject of the world's largest three-dimensional sculpture, located in the Black Hills of South Dakota, seven miles away from Mount Rushmore.

∘°ₒ°○∘

Mount Rushmore, named for a New York lawyer, was sculpted by Danish-American Gutzon Borglum and his son, Lincoln.

═══ COVER ART ═══
7 POINTS

Spencer Elden is the name of the baby on Nirvana's ***Nevermind*** album (1991).

Andy Warhol created the album covers for **The Velvet Underground & Nico** (1967) and The Rolling Stones's **Sticky Fingers** (1971).

The Beatles's **Sgt. Pepper's Lonely Hearts Club Band** (1967) included seventy people on the cover, including Edgar Allen Poe, Bob Dylan, Sonny Liston, and Shirley Temple (twice).

Blind Faith released a self-titled album in 1969 with a topless pubescent girl on the cover holding a silver winged object. The controversial cover was photographed by Bob Seidemann; the girl, Mariora Goschen, was reported to be eleven years old.

The cover of Pink Floyd's **The Dark Side of the Moon** (1973), which features a prism, was selected for preservation in the United States by the National Recording Registry of the Library of Congress, who "[deemed] it culturally, historically, or aesthetically significant."

Elvis Presley's debut album (1956) features "the King" performing at the Fort Homer Hesterly Armory in Tampa, Florida. The Clash mimicked the album cover for their album *London Calling*.

The Clash album **London Calling** (1979) features bassist Paul Simonon smashing his Fender bass against the stage at The Palladium in New York City. The photograph by Pennie Smith was named the best rock and roll photograph of all time by *Q* magazine in 2002.

∘°∘°O∘

U2's **War** features a boy on the cover. That boy is Peter Rowen, the brother of Bono's friend.

∘°∘°O∘

The Who's **Tommy** (1969) features a sphere of clouds and seagulls with diamond-shaped cutouts.

∘°∘°O∘

Jane's Addiction's **Nothing's Shocking** (1988) features a pair of nude conjoined twin women sitting on a sideways rocking chair with their heads on fire. It was created by band leader Perry Farrell, who used his girlfriend as the model in the casting.

∘°∘°O∘

Led Zeppelin's self-titled debut album (1969) features a black and white image of the Hindenburg seconds after it caught fire.

∘°∘°O∘

Big Brother and the Holding Company's **Cheap Thrills** (1968) album cover, featuring Janis Joplin, was drawn by cartoonist Robert Crumb.

There's no need to memorize every style of painting and every artist, but if you know a few major artists and the general time periods, you should do well with any questions that bring up art styles and movements.

- Baroque (seventeenth century): Peter Paul Rubens, Caravaggio
- Romanticism (eighteenth century): William Blake, J.M.W. Turner
- Impressionism (nineteenth century): Claude Monet, Pierre-Auguste Renoir
- Pointillism (nineteenth century): Georges Seurat, Vincent van Gogh
- Dada (twentieth century): Man Ray, Marcel Duchamp
- Fauvism (twentieth century): Henri Matisse, André Derain
- Cubism (twentieth century): Pablo Picasso, Paul Cezanne
- Surrealism (twentieth century): Salvador Dali, René Magritte
- American Modernism (twentieth century): Georgia O'Keeffe, Aaron Douglas
- Abstract Impressionism (twentieth century): Jackson Pollock, Willem de Kooning
- Pop Art (twentieth century): Andy Warhol, Roy Lichtenstein

The cover of the album **Ooh La La** by Faces (1973) features "Gas-tone," a character from the 1920s played by Italian comedian Ettore Petrolini.

∘°∘°○∘

The Doors's **Strange Days** (1967) features dwarfs, a trumpeter, and a juggler in a New York City alley. The Doors band members only appear in a poster in the background.

CHAPTER 9

SCIENCE

Do you know . . .

- What is the longest bone in the human body?
- Which animal has four knees?
- What is the largest member of the dolphin family?
- Who invented bifocal glasses?
- What is the only letter not to appear on the Periodic Table of elements?

Can't figure out the answers to these questions? You're not alone. Since the beginning of time, humans have struggled to make sense of this crazy world we live in. In an effort to understand, humans have attempted to categorize anything and everything from the human body, plants and animals, physics, elements, technology, and more. Our preoccupation with all things science makes this topic a frequent trivia category, and not just because it's fun to yell "*Science!*" Thomas Dolby–style. The good thing is that if you know a little about science, the answers are usually pretty guessable. To be solid, you need to be familiar with the facts found in this chapter, including the Periodic Table; have a working knowledge of some of the major bones; and understand some of the basics—think eighth grade science: photosynthesis, mitosis, and gravity.

THE HUMAN BODY
1 POINT

There are 206 bones in the human body. The **femur**, or the thighbone, is the longest. The stirrup, located in the ear, is the smallest.

$$\circ \,{}^{\circ}{}_{\circ}{}^{\circ} O \circ$$

The **pineal gland** in the brain is the smallest organ in the human body, followed by the parathyroid gland, then the pituitary, which produces HGH, human growth hormone.

$$\circ \,{}^{\circ}{}_{\circ}{}^{\circ} O \circ$$

The **liver** is the largest gland in the human body, the aorta is the largest artery, and the sciatic is the longest nerve.

$$\circ \,{}^{\circ}{}_{\circ}{}^{\circ} O \circ$$

The pancreas produces **insulin**, a hormone that helps the body metabolize glucose. "Insulin" is derived from the Latin word *insula*, which means "island."

$$\circ \,{}^{\circ}{}_{\circ}{}^{\circ} O \circ$$

Humans have thirty-two permanent **teeth**. Tooth enamel is the hardest substance in the human body.

$$\circ \,{}^{\circ}{}_{\circ}{}^{\circ} O \circ$$

The four **lobes** of the brain are the:
- Frontal, which regulates decision making and problem solving
- Parietal, which processes sensory information
- Occipital, which processes visual stimulation
- Temporal, which regulates memory, learning, hearing, and language

。°o°O。

Rabies (the word is derived from the Latin for "madness") causes acute encephalitis (inflammation of the brain) in warm-blooded animals.

。°o°O。

Forty-six, or twenty-three pairs, of **chromosomes** are in the human body. The four DNA base pairs are: guanine, cytosine, adenine, and thymine.

。°o°O。

In 1950, the **kidney** was the first human organ to be successfully transplanted. In 1967 in South Africa, Dr. Christiaan Barnard became the first surgeon to successfully perform a human heart transplant.

。°o°O。

Based on the studies of Dr. Duncan MacDougall in the early 1900s, "three-fourths of an ounce" (later referred to as "21 grams") is the weight that is lost when a body dies. MacDougall believed this was the weight of the **human soul**.

UNITS NAMED FOR SCIENTISTS

Ever wonder where the unusual names of some units of measurement came from? Check out this list and drop the info like a pro the next time someone asks you which scientist lent his name to a unit of energy. It *will* come up. Trust me.

- Joule: energy, work, heat (James Prescott Joule)
- Volt: electric potential (Allessandro Volta)
- Ampere: electric current (André-Marie Ampère)
- Hertz: frequency (Heinrich Hertz)
- Tesla: magnetic flux (Nikola Tesla)
- Kelvin: thermodynamic temperature (Lord Kelvin)
- Ohm: electric resistance (Georg Ohm)
- Becquerel: radioactivity (Henri Becquerel)
- Weber: magnetic flux (Wilhelm Weber)
- Newton: force (Isaac Newton)

The **masseter muscle** in the jaw is the strongest muscle in the human body. The gluteus maximus (sometimes known as the badonkadonk) is the largest muscle.

∘°ₒ°○∘

Collagen is the most abundant protein in the human body. Among other things, it works to hold the epidermis (skin) together.

∘°ₒ°○∘

James Watson and Francis Crick discovered the double helix structure of **DNA** in 1953. Crick's wife, Odile, originally created the iconic drawing of this structure.

THE ANIMAL KINGDOM
3 POINTS

Traveling at speeds of one or two miles per hour, a **sloth** is the slowest mammal. The cheetah is the world's fastest mammal.

○°○°○○

Sleeping twenty-two hours a day, **koalas** are the laziest animals in the world. Eucalyptus leaves make up 99 percent of their diet. The word *koala* comes from the aboriginal term for "no drink."

○°○°○○

Sperm whales have the largest brain of any animal that has ever been known to live.

○°○°○○

The **orca** is the largest member of the dolphin family.

○°○°○○

The **giant squid** has larger eyes than any other animal.

The **blue whale** is believed to be the largest animal ever to have lived. The world's smallest mammals are the bumblebee bat of Thailand and the Etruscan shrew.

∘ᵒ∘ᵒ∘

Eighty percent of all animal species belong to the phylum **Arthropoda**, which includes insects, arachnids, and crustaceans.

∘ᵒ∘ᵒ∘

The **praying mantis** is the only insect that can turn its head like a human, allowing some species nearly 300 degrees of movement.

∘ᵒ∘ᵒ∘

The venomous **tarantula** is named for the city where it once thrived, Taranto, Italy.

∘ᵒ∘ᵒ∘

Guppies are named after Robert John Lechmere Guppy, who was thought to have first discovered them in Trinidad in 1866.

∘ᵒ∘ᵒ∘

Giraffes are the only animals born with horns. They have the longest tails of any land mammal, and the highest known blood pressure.

∘ᵒ∘ᵒ∘

Asian elephants on average live up to eighty years in captivity and sixty years in the wild. Elephants are also the only animals with four knees.

$_\circ{}^{\circ}_{\circ}{}^{\circ}\!\circ{}_\circ$

Most **hamsters** that people keep as pets today originate from a litter found in Syria in 1930. Their name comes from the German for "to hoard food," as that is what they do.

$_\circ{}^{\circ}_{\circ}{}^{\circ}\!\circ{}_\circ$

South America's **capybara** is the world's largest rodent. The beaver is the largest rodent in North America, followed by the porcupine.

$_\circ{}^{\circ}_{\circ}{}^{\circ}\!\circ{}_\circ$

Galapagos tortoises have the longest life span of any animal on Earth, living up to 170 years.

$_\circ{}^{\circ}_{\circ}{}^{\circ}\!\circ{}_\circ$

Gorilla is the only genus that is also the name of the animal.

$_\circ{}^{\circ}_{\circ}{}^{\circ}\!\circ{}_\circ$

The birds with the longest wingspans are:
1. **Wandering albatross** (12 feet)
2. **White pelican** (11.8 feet)
3. **Marabou stork** (10.5 feet)
4. **Andean condor** (10.5 feet)
5. **Whooping swan** (9.8 feet)
6. **Bearded vulture** (9.3 feet)

Cranes are the world's tallest flying birds.

The last confirmed sighting of a **dodo bird** was in 1662 on the island of Mauritius.

THE GREAT BARRIER REEF

Humans aren't the only architects in nature. The Great Barrier Reef, located in the Coral Sea off the northeastern coast of Australia, is the largest structure ever built up by living creatures. It contains more than 2,900 individual reefs and 900 islands across more than 1,400 miles, and covers an area of more than 130,000 square miles. It can be seen from outer space and is made up of a billion tiny coral polyps, named because they have a passing resemblance to teeny octopi.

The **Irish wolfhound** is considered to be the tallest dog.

The four big cat species in the genus *panthera* that are capable of roaring are the **tiger**, **lion**, **jaguar**, and **leopard**. The puma, cheetah, and snow leopard cannot roar.

The **kiwi** is the only bird to have nostrils at the tip of its bill. It is the national bird of New Zealand.

∘°ₒ°O∘

Canada is home to more than half of the world's population of **bald eagles**. In the United States, Florida and Minnesota contain the largest populations of America's national bird.

∘°ₒ°O∘

The **monarch butterfly** has the longest migration route of any butterfly species.

∘°ₒ°O∘

The **great white shark** has killed more humans than any other shark. The tiger shark comes in second.

∘°ₒ°O∘

The only egg-laying mammals are the **duck-billed platypus** and two species of echidna, or "spiny anteaters." The platypus is one of only a few venomous mammals.

∘°ₒ°O∘

The Galapagos Islands contain the only **cormorants** that are flightless. These islands also contain the most northerly penguins of the seventeen species, all of which are found below the equator.

ELEMENTS, SYMBOLS, AND ATOMIC NUMBERS

5 POINTS

The letter **J** is the only letter that doesn't appear on the Periodic Table of elements.

Hydrogen (H, 1) makes up approximately 90 percent of the known universe.

Titanium (Ti, 22) is found in almost all living things, rocks, water bodies, and soils.

Mercury (Hg, 80) is the only metallic element that is liquid at room temperature.

Curium (Cm, 96) is the only element that is named for a married couple: Marie and Pierre Curie.

Lithium (Li, 3) is the lightest of all solid elements.

○ ○ ○ ○ ○

Platinum (Pt, 78) is one of the rarest elements in the Earth's crust.

○ ○ ○ ○ ○

Carbon (C, 6) is a girl's best friend, as it is the basis of diamonds—in addition to close to ten million other known compounds.

○ ○ ○ ○ ○

Plutonium (Pu, 94) is the most toxic of all metals. Dr. Glenn Seaborg, who first discovered it, called it "Pu" as a joke.

○ ○ ○ ○ ○

Aluminum (Al, 13) makes up 8 percent of the Earth's crust, making it the most abundant metallic element there.

○ ○ ○ ○ ○

Lead (Pb, 82)—known in Latin as *plumbum* (hence: Pb)—is the heaviest nonradioactive element.

○ ○ ○ ○ ○

Uranium (U, 92) is the heaviest naturally occurring element.

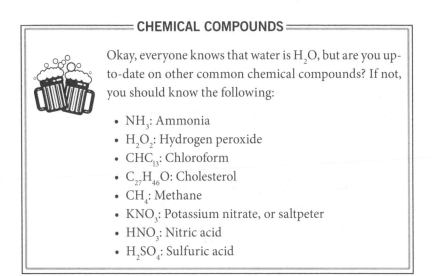

CHEMICAL COMPOUNDS

Okay, everyone knows that water is H_2O, but are you up-to-date on other common chemical compounds? If not, you should know the following:

- NH_3: Ammonia
- H_2O_2: Hydrogen peroxide
- CHC_{13}: Chloroform
- $C_{27}H_{46}O$: Cholesterol
- CH_4: Methane
- KNO_3: Potassium nitrate, or saltpeter
- HNO_3: Nitric acid
- H_2SO_4: Sulfuric acid

Helium (He, 2) makes up 24 percent of the sun's mass. Hydrogen makes up 74 percent.

$_\circ{}^{O}{}_{O}{}^{\circ}O\circ$

Silver (Ag, 47) has the highest electrical conductivity of any element and the highest thermal conductivity of any metal.

$_\circ{}^{O}{}_{O}{}^{\circ}O\circ$

Silicon (Si, 14) is the second most abundant element in the Earth's crust after Oxygen (O, 8).

$_\circ{}^{O}{}_{O}{}^{\circ}O\circ$

Oxygen was discovered by Joseph Priestley in 1774 but was named by Antoine Lavoisier in 1777.

INVENTIONS
7 POINTS

Dr. Harry Coover developed **Super Glue**, or **Krazy Glue**, originally called Eastman 910, in 1942 while working for Kodak.

○ °○° ○ ○

Cockleburs inspired the invention of **Velcro** by George de Mestral in 1941.

○ °○° ○ ○

Vulcanization, named for the Roman god of fire, is the chemical process for converting rubber into more durable materials.

○ °○° ○ ○

Norm Larsen invented **WD-40** in 1953. "WD" stands for "water displacement," and the "40" is because Larsen finally gained success on his fortieth attempt.

○ °○° ○ ○

Some **acronyms** you should know:
- scuba—self-contained underwater breathing apparatus
- EKG—electrocardiogram
- BTU—British thermal unit
- PVC–polyvinyl chloride
- laser—light amplification by stimulated emission of radiation
- USB—universal serial bus

- HTTP—hypertext transfer protocol
- URL—uniform resource locator

∘°₀°O∘

Martin Cooper invented the **cell phone** in the 1970s, and was the first to use it in public.

∘°₀°O∘

Psychologist William Marston, inventor of the **polygraph**, or lie detector, also created Wonder Woman (1941), who was equipped with a Lasso of Truth.

∘°₀°O∘

Important **names and dates** in invention:
- Printing press (1450)—Johannes Gutenberg
- Magnifying lens (1520)—Roger Bacon
- Mercury thermometer (1724)—Daniel Gabriel Fahrenheit
- Steam engine (1781)—James Watt
- Metric system (1790)—France
- Cotton gin (1793)—Eli Whitney
- Telegraph (1837)—Samuel Morse
- Sewing machine (1846)—Elias Howe
- Antiseptic surgery (1865)—Joseph Lister
- Dynamite (1867)—Alfred Nobel
- Periodic Table of elements (1871)—Dmitri Mendeleev
- Fountain pen (1884)—L.E. Waterman
- Motorcycle (1885)—Gottlieb Daimler
- Aspirin (1899)—Dr. Felix Hoffmann
- Frozen food (1925)—Clarence Birdseye

- Geodesic dome (1926)—Buckminster Fuller
- TV remote control (1955)—Zenith
- Three-point seat belt (1959)—Volvo
- Supercomputer (1964)—Seymour Cray

₀°ₒ°O°

Benjamin Franklin invented the lightning rod, bifocal glasses, a map of the Gulf Stream, a carriage odometer, swim fins, the catheter, daylight saving time, and the Franklin stove.

₀°ₒ°O°

Leonardo da Vinci invented ball bearings, a parachute, a diving suit, the machine gun, the armored tank, and a flying machine.

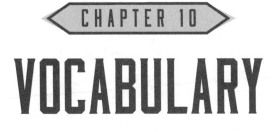

VOCABULARY

Do you know . . .

- What insect provides the origin of nitpick?
- What beverage comes from the French meaning "without caffeine"?
- Which British admiral first used the term "OMG" in 1917?
- What word, a recurring theme in this book, means "a junction of three roads"?
- After which Greek nymph was Jacques Cousteau's research ship named?

If you're not sure of the answers to these questions, it's time to break open the dictionary and brush up on your vocabulary . . . or you could just take a look through the facts in this chapter. Vocabulary is actually one of the most fun trivia categories. Words have the most interesting origins, whether they are derived from other languages, named for people, or simply made up. Though preparing for this category may feel like studying for the SATs, keep in mind that a working knowledge of Latin and Greek roots can give you those few points you need to win the whole thing.

DOUBLE MEANING
1 POINT

Sanguine means "cheerfully optimistic" and also describes a reddish-brown chalk used in art. This word gets its meaning from the Latin word for "blood."

∘°∘°○∘

Accolade is "an honor or expression of praise," and is also the proper term to describe the touch on someone's shoulders with the flat blade of a sword in the ceremony to confer knighthood.

∘°∘°○∘

The word **nitpick** can mean to criticize unnecessarily. It also describes the actual process of removing lice from someone's head. The first one sounds better, thank you very much.

∘°∘°○∘

From the Spanish word for "pirate," **filibuster** was first used in the United States to describe the legislative delay in 1854 during discussions concerning the Kansas-Nebraska Act.

∘°∘°○∘

Vermiform means "worm-shaped" and is also used to describe the human appendix.

Growler is used to define icebergs that are less than 3.3 feet high and less than 16 feet long. It is also the name for a bottle made to contain sixty-four ounces of beer.

Shambles refers to a scene of destruction, and is the name of the workstation used by a butcher.

An **apron** is a frock to be worn in the kitchen, and it also refers to the area of a boxing or wrestling ring that extends between one and two feet beyond the ropes.

Serendipity is an old name for what is now called Sri Lanka because in a fairy tale set there, people "were always making discoveries . . . of things they were not in quest of."

Trivia, the subject of this best book ever, also means "a junction of three roads."

Calypso is the name of the nymph who enticed Odysseus into a cave for seven years, and it's also a type of music that originates in Trinidad and Tobago. *Calypso* is also the name of Jacques Cousteau's research ship.

═══ ORIGINS ═══
3 POINTS

Meandering can mean "rambling," and derives from the name of a river located in present-day Turkey that features a very convoluted path with several turns.

∘°o°O°∘

According to Pliny the Elder, the word **salary** comes from the Roman practice of paying soldiers with salt.

∘°o°O°∘

King Pine trees were reserved for the British Empire as ship masts. The term **windfall** originates from King Pines that came down naturally and could legally be used by the locals.

∘°o°O°∘

Bedlam derives from the nickname of the first asylum for the insane in England, the Hospital of St. Mary of Bethlehem.

∘°o°O°∘

Deriving from the Greek for "little sail," **vexillology** is the study of flags.

∘°ₒ°O∘

Pundit originates from the Sanskrit word for "learned," referring to someone who conducted religious ceremonies and offered counsel to the king.

∘°ₒ°O∘

A **glitch** is a computer mishap, stemming from the Yiddish word for "slip."

∘°ₒ°O∘

The term **sabbatical** originates from the ancient Israelite practice of letting fields lie fallow every seventh year.

∘°ₒ°O∘

Macramé is a form of textile making derived from the Arabic word for "striped towel." It was introduced to the West by the court of Queen Mary in the late seventeenth century.

∘°ₒ°O∘

Some common English words with foreign-language origins include:
- **Yogurt**—Turkish
- **Geyser**—Icelandic
- **Mattress**—Arabic
- **Sauna**—Finnish

∘°ₒ°O∘

A **geek** is a carnival performer billed as a wild man whose act includes biting the head off a live chicken or snake.

○ ○ ○ ○ ○

Italics is named for Italy and is based on a Renaissance script.

=== IT'S ALL GREEK TO ME ===

These are some common English words that derive from Greek words and their original meanings:

- Herpes: "creeping"
- Sarcasm: "to tear the flesh"
- Photosynthesis: "light" and "putting together"
- Diamond: "unbreakable"
- Sarcophagus: "flesh-eating stone"
- Isosceles: "with equal legs"
- Psychedelic: "mind" and "visible"

Pumpernickel bread comes from the German meaning "to create gas in the bowels of the Devil."

○ ○ ○ ○ ○

Panko is derived from the Portuguese word for "bread" and a Japanese suffix indicating "crumb" or "powder."

○ ○ ○ ○ ○

Sanka comes from the French word for "without caffeine." **Cappuccino** is the Italian word for "hood," named for and invented by Italian monks.

◦O◦°O◦

The **peace symbol** is a combination of the semaphore signals for the letters "N" and "D" for "nuclear disarmament."

COINING WORDS AND PHRASES
5 POINTS

Franz Anton Mesmer coined the term **animal magnetism** in 1774, and is named in the word "mesmerize."

◦O◦°O◦

Gerrymander was first used by the *Boston Gazette* in 1812. The governor of Massachusetts, Elbridge Gerry, had changed the election district to the shape of a salamander, giving him an unfair advantage over challengers.

◦O◦°O◦

Millionaire was coined in 1843 by a newspaper reporter in an obituary of Pierre Lorillard.

◦O◦°O◦

Boycott is named for the absentee English landlord Charles Boycott (1832–1897), whom the Irish refused to deal with.

∘°∘°∘∘

Vaseline was invented in 1872 by Robert Chesebrough, coining the name from the German for "water" and the Greek for "oil."

∘°∘°∘∘

Lunatic fringe was coined by President Teddy Roosevelt in his review of the 1913 Exhibition of Modern Art, better known as the Armory Show.

∘°∘°∘∘

OMG was first used in a letter written by Lord Fisher, a naval admiral, to Winston Churchill in 1917.

∘°∘°∘∘

James Hilton coined **Shangri-la** in his book *Lost Horizon* (1933).

∘°∘°∘∘

Ever wonder who came up with some of the more "scientific" terms that you need to know on trivia night? Here, you'll find a response to anyone who's ever said, "Talk nerdy to me!"

- **Android** (1270)—Albertus Magnus
- **Robot** (1921)—Karel Capek
- **Quantum foam** and **wormhole**—John Archibald Wheeler
- **Big bang** (1950)—Sir Fred Hoyle

Franklin Delano Roosevelt first used the term **United Nations** in a 1942 declaration.

∘°ₒ°O∘

Winston Churchill first used the term **iron curtain** in 1946.

∘°ₒ°O∘

Dancer and actor Mr. Bojangles (Bill Robinson), who appeared in films with Shirley Temple in the 1930s, coined the term **copacetic**, meaning "in excellent order."

∘°ₒ°O∘

Donald Watson coined the word **vegan**—"a vegetarian who eats no butter, eggs, cheese or milk"—in 1944 in England. Followers of the diet include Alec Baldwin, Bill Clinton, and Ellen DeGeneres.

∘°ₒ°O∘

Nam June Paik of South Korea, considered a founder of video arts, coined the term **information superhighway** in 1974.

∘°ₒ°O∘

Metrosexual was first seen in an article by Mark Simpson titled "Here come the mirror men," *The Independent*, November 1994.

∘°ₒ°O∘

Stephen Colbert coined the term **truthiness**, the *New York Times* Word of the Year for 2005.

MILITARY SPEAK
7 POINTS

Jeep comes from the abbreviation "G.P.," which in military terminology stands for a "general purpose" vehicle.

∘°ₒ°O∘

The whole nine yards originally referred to the length of machine gun ammo belts used by fighter pilots during WWII: twenty-seven feet long. If pilots fired all of their ammo, the targets got "the whole nine yards."

∘°ₒ°O∘

SNAFU is an acronym for "Situation Normal: All Fouled Up."

∘°ₒ°O∘

The term **basket case**, which is used to describe someone beyond help, originates from a description of WWI soldiers who had lost both arms and both legs in battle.

∘°ₒ°O∘

Concentration camp was coined in 1900 during the Boer War.

Honcho comes from the word for a Japanese squad commander.

The word **decimate** derives from the Roman army's practice of having one of every ten soldiers beaten to death by the other nine. *Decem* means "ten" in Latin.

Sabotage comes from the French for "wooden shoe," as disgruntled French workers would throw their wooden clogs into machinery during the Industrial Revolution.

Curfew comes from the Old French for "cover the fire."

Military contractors refer to a hammer as a **manually powered fastener-driving impact device**. A pencil is a **portable hand-held communications inscriber**.

Taken from the phonetic alphabet, the military uses the term **Zulu** for Coordinated Universal Time or Greenwich Mean Time.

Broken arrow in military terms refers to losing an atomic bomb, which first happened in British Columbia in 1950. John Travolta and Christian Slater starred in the film *Broken Arrow* (1996).

$_\circ{}^{\circ}\!{}_{\circ}{}^{\circ}{\large\text{O}}{}^{\circ}{}_\circ$

Alamo is Spanish for **cottonwood**.

$_\circ{}^{\circ}\!{}_{\circ}{}^{\circ}{\large\text{O}}{}^{\circ}{}_\circ$

E pluribus unum—**Out of many, one**—is a phrase that appears on the Seal of the United States. This term is attributed to the Roman poet Virgil, who used it to describe the lunch of a simple farmer who grinds cheese, garlic, and herbs together in a ball.

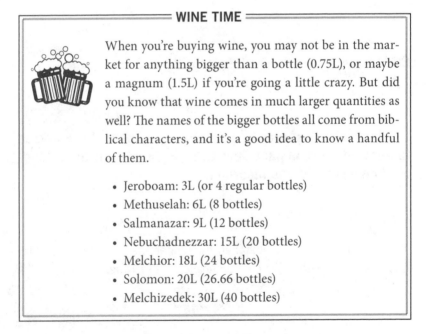

=== **WINE TIME** ===

When you're buying wine, you may not be in the market for anything bigger than a bottle (0.75L), or maybe a magnum (1.5L) if you're going a little crazy. But did you know that wine comes in much larger quantities as well? The names of the bigger bottles all come from biblical characters, and it's a good idea to know a handful of them.

- Jeroboam: 3L (or 4 regular bottles)
- Methuselah: 6L (8 bottles)
- Salmanazar: 9L (12 bottles)
- Nebuchadnezzar: 15L (20 bottles)
- Melchior: 18L (24 bottles)
- Solomon: 20L (26.66 bottles)
- Melchizedek: 30L (40 bottles)

SPORTS AND BUSINESS

ROUND 3

SPORTS

Do you know . . .

- Which Major League Baseball (MLB) player holds the record for consecutive games played?
- Who kicked the longest field goal?
- What NBA coach coined the term "three-peat"?
- What team was the center of "Spygate" in 2007?
- Who is the only individual to be named *Sports Illustrated* Sportsman of the Year twice?

If you don't know the answers, don't feel bad. Throughout history, there have been a lot of sports, a lot of players, and a lot of records. After all, sports is arguably the oldest form of entertainment (excluding you know what). It's tough to remember a vast amount of sports trivia, but you can make sure you know the important facts by flipping through this chapter. The odds are there will be at least one (if not more) sports questions in every pub quiz because, well, these trivia games are held in bars where televised sports are often playing at the same time. If you want to experience the thrill of victory, you will need someone on your team who knows a lot of sports facts. Otherwise, be prepared to face the agony of defeat.

HALL OF FAMERS

1 POINT

Babe Ruth, the first player to hit fifty home runs in back to back seasons, was born George Herman Ruth in Baltimore, Maryland, in 1895. After the 1919 season, the popular legend is that Ruth was sold to the New York Yankees by Red Sox owner Harry Frazee to fund a theater play called *No, No, Nanette*, but this has since been debunked. In 1936, Ruth became an inaugural member of the Baseball Hall of Fame, along with Honus Wagner, Walter Johnson, and Ty Cobb.

In 1934, **Lou Gehrig** became the first athlete depicted on a Wheaties box. But his impressive achievements didn't stop there. Gehrig's #4 jersey was the first number to be retired in all of sports, on July 4, 1939, and he was the leader in career grand slams (twenty-three) until 2013, when Alex Rodriguez scored his twenty-fourth. Gehrig died from ALS (amyotrophic lateral sclerosis), or Lou Gehrig's Disease, in 1941 at the age of thirty-seven.

Ted Williams, a two-time Triple Crown winner, had the highest career on-base-percentage average at .482. He was also the last MLB player to bat over .400 in a season. Williams left the major leagues for three years in 1943 to fight in WWII. Upon returning from war in 1946, Williams earned his first Most Valuable Player (MVP) award and made his only World Series appearance.

African American players were not allowed in the major leagues until 1947. **Jackie Robinson** is credited as the first, playing for the Brooklyn Dodgers. Born in January 1919, the month Teddy Roosevelt died, Robinson was given the middle name Roosevelt.

○ ○ ○ ○ ○

Roberto Clemente hit exactly 3,000 hits before his untimely death in a plane crash on New Year's Eve in 1972, at the age of thirty-eight. The 6th Street Bridge in Pittsburgh is also known as the Roberto Clemente Bridge, in his honor.

○ ○ ○ ○ ○

Rickey Henderson holds the record for most stolen bases (1,406), times caught stealing (335), runs scored (2,295), leadoff home runs (81), and unintentional walks (2,129).

○ ○ ○ ○ ○

Jackie Robinson, **Roberto Clemente**, **Lou Gehrig**, and **Babe Ruth** were the first four MLB players to appear on U.S. postage stamps.

○ ○ ○ ○ ○

Hakeem Olajuwon is the only NBA player to win the MVP, Defensive Player of the Year, and Finals MVP awards in the same year (1994). Sam Bowie and Olajuwon were both drafted ahead of #3 pick Michael Jordan in 1984.

Michael Jordan holds the record for most seasons leading the NBA in scoring (ten). He has also appeared on a Wheaties box more times than any other athlete (eighteen).

Larry Bird is the only NBA MVP to be named Coach of the Year, and Executive of the Year.

Bobby Orr won the Norris Trophy for best defensive hockey player every year from 1968 to 1975, and became the youngest player to be inducted into the Hockey Hall of Fame in 1979 at the age of thirty-one.

Mark Messier is the only player in any professional sport to captain two different teams to a championship win, the Stanley Cup in this case. He did it five times for the Edmonton Oilers and once with the New York Rangers.

Of all players in North American men's sports leagues, **Wayne Gretzky** has won the most MVP awards (nine). His uniform #99 was retired throughout the National Hockey League (NHL). The only other player to have his number retired throughout an entire league is Jackie Robinson (#42).

Three people have been inducted into the **Naismith Memorial Basketball Hall of Fame** as both a player and a coach: John Wooden (1973), Bill Sharman (2004), and Lenny Wilkens (2004).

RECORDS AND AWARDS
3 POINTS

Bobby Jones founded and helped design the Augusta National Golf Club, which hosts the Masters each year. In 1930, he became the first man to sweep golf's four Grand Slam tournament championships: U.S. Open, U.S. Amateur, British Open, and British Amateur. Today a Grand Slam would mean wins at the Masters, U.S. Open, British Open, and Pacific Golfers' Association (PGA) tournaments.

In 1964, **Arnold Palmer** became the first four-time Masters golf champion.

Three golfers have won the Masters tournament in consecutive years: **Jack Nicklaus** (1965, 1966), **Nick Faldo** (1989, 1990), and **Tiger Woods** (2001, 2002). Three golfers have won in their Major debut: Francis Ouimet (who inspired the film *The Greatest Game Ever*

Played)—U.S. Open (1913); Ben Curtis—British Open (2003); and Keegan Bradley—PGA Championship (2011).

∘°₀°○∘

Brazil has won the most World Cups (five), followed by Italy (four), Germany (three), Argentina (two), Uruguay (two), France (one), England (one), and Spain (one).

∘°₀°○∘

In 1975, **Fred Lynn**, after his first year with the Boston Red Sox, became the only player to win the Rookie of the Year award and MVP in the same season. Lynn was a college roommate with Pittsburgh Steelers wide receiver and Super Bowl X MVP, Lynn Swann.

∘°₀°○∘

Hall of Famer **Cal Ripken Jr.** broke Lou Gehrig's fifty-six-year-old record for consecutive games played (2,130) in 1995. Ripken was also the first player to win Rookie of the Year (1982) and MVP (1983) in consecutive seasons. Others to accomplish this are Ichiro Suzuki, Ryan Howard, and Dustin Pedroia.

∘°₀°○∘

The longest game in professional baseball was played between two Triple-A teams: the **Pawtucket Red Sox** and the **Rochester Red Wings** at McCoy Stadium in Rhode Island. The game began on April 18, 1981 and, still tied up, was suspended on April 19th just after 4 A.M. at the end of the thirty-second inning. The thirty-third inning was played on June 23rd. After eight hours and twenty-five minutes of total playing time, Pawtucket finally won with a 3–2 score over the Red Wings.

∘°ₒ°O∘

Trevor Hoffman was the first MLB pitcher to reach 500 and 600 career saves, and held the record for the most until 2011, when Mariano Rivera beat his record. Francisco Rodriguez (K-Rod) holds the record for most saves in a single season (sixty-two), ahead of Bobby Thigpen (fifty-five).

∘°ₒ°O∘

Aroldis Chapman of the Cincinnati Reds set the MLB record for the fastest recorded pitch in September 2010 at 105.1 mph.

∘°ₒ°O∘

LaDainian Tomlinson, who played for the San Diego Chargers, holds the record for the most single season touchdowns (thirty-one). The previous record (twenty-eight) was set in 2005 by Shaun Alexander of the Seattle Seahawks.

∘°ₒ°O∘

The cities that have hosted the most **Super Bowls** are Miami (ten), New Orleans (ten), Los Angeles (seven), and Tampa (four).

∘°ₒ°O∘

Quarterbacks **Terry Bradshaw**, **Roger Staubach**, **Joe Namath**, **Tom Brady**, and **Aaron Rodgers** all wore #12 jerseys during a winning Super Bowl game.

∘°∘°○∘

In 2013, **Matt Prater** set a National Football League (NFL) record with a sixty-four-yard field goal. Tom Dempsey (Saints, 1970), Jason Elam (Broncos, 1998), Sebastian Janikowski (Raiders, 2011), and David Akers (49ers, 2012) have all kicked sixty-three yarders.

∘°∘°○∘

Ben Wallace and **Dikembe Mutombo** have won NBA's Defensive Player of the Year Award the most times (four). Hakeem Olajuwon has the most blocked shots (3,830), followed by Dikembe Mutombo (3,289) and Kareem Abdul-Jabbar (3,189).

∘°∘°○∘

Cale Yarborough (1976–1978) won three consecutive NASCAR Cup Series championships. Jimmie Johnson won five in a row (2006–2010). Johnson is the first racing driver to become the Associated Press Male Athlete of the Year (2009).

∘°∘°○∘

The fastest ball game in sports is **Jai Alai**, with the ball reaching speeds of up to 188 mph. The name of the game comes from the Basque term for "basket tip." The ball is called a "pelota" and the court is called a "fronton."

°O°O°

Spencer Gore was the first winner of Wimbledon (1877). Pete Sampras (1993–1995, 1997–2000) and Roger Federer (2003–2007, 2009, 2012) have won the most Wimbledon men's singles championships (seven).

°O°O°

Clocked at 163.4 mph in 2013, **Samuel Groth** of Australia holds the record for the fastest serve in tennis, a record formerly owned by American Andy Roddick.

°O°O°

In 2013, at the age of thirty-one, **Serena Williams** became the oldest top-ranked woman ever in singles tennis. At the age of forty-six, Martina Navratilova was the oldest player to win a Tennis Grand Slam title, which was for mixed doubles at both the Australian Open and Wimbledon in 2003.

°O°O°

Bobby and Brett Hull and **Jean-Paul and Zach Parise** are the two fathers and sons who have each scored 200 or more NHL goals.

°O°O°

The **Stanley Cup** is the oldest trophy competed for in North America (1893).

Three-peat is a portmanteau of *three* and *repeat*, trademarked by NBA coach Pat Riley. In 1993, the Chicago Bulls were the first team to three-peat (that is, earn three back-to-back championships). Until 2003, Riley was paid royalties whenever the term was used.

∘°∘°O∘

Chick Hearn, the play-by-play announcer for the Los Angeles Lakers, broadcasted 3,338 consecutive games during a career that started in 1965. Hearn invented a few colorful phrases during his tenure, including **slam dunk**, **air ball**, and **no harm, no foul**.

∘°∘°O∘

Football coach Vince Lombardi coined the term **game plan**. Lombardi was the coach of the Green Bay Packers, and he led his team to victories in the first two Super Bowls (1966 and 1967). Born in Brooklyn, he had previously coached the Giants (1954–1958).

∘°∘°O∘

The football term **sack** was coined by Deacon Jones, a 1980 Pro Football Hall of Fame inductee. Nicknamed "the Secretary of Defense," Jones was called the "most valuable Ram of all time" by the *Los Angeles Times*.

o°o°O o

Hail Mary was coined by Roger Staubach, a Heisman Trophy winner (1963) who spent his entire career on the Dallas Cowboys (1969–1979). The term was named after a pass that Staubach threw in a 1975 playoff game against the Minnesota Vikings. Staubach later said he prayed a "Hail Mary" after throwing the fifty-yard bomb to Drew Pearson. Dallas earned the victory that day, 17–14.

o°o°O o

Hat trick is a term used for scoring three times in a game. It was first used in an 1858 cricket match to describe HH Stephenson's feat of taking three wickets with three consecutive deliveries. This term is commonly used in hockey, and Wayne Gretzky holds the hat trick record with fifty-two.

o°o°O o

Southpaw is a slang term for a left-handed athlete. The term originates from baseball when ball diamonds were often laid out so that the batters faced east, to avoid looking into the afternoon sun. The pitcher's left hand, or paw, would therefore be on the southern side. The term was coined by a Chicago journalist in 1887.

o°o°O o

Bill James is a baseball writer, historian, and statistician who popularized the term **moneyball**. Through *sabermetrics*, coined by James, baseball numbers are scientifically analyzed and applied to produce more wins with less revenue. *Moneyball: The Art of Winning an Unfair Game* (2003) is a book by Michael Lewis about the Oakland Athletics and General Manager Billy Beane. This book was adapted to an Oscar-nominated Brad Pitt film in 2011.

$\circ\,^{\circ}_{\circ}{}^{\circ}\mathrm{O}\circ$

The **high five** was coined and first displayed by Dodgers outfielders Glenn Burke and Dusty Baker on October 2, 1977.

WHO WERE THEY NAMED FOR?

You can see where some sports terms come from—easy examples include a home run (baseball), a slam dunk (basketball), and a hole in one (golf). Their sources are just as they sound. But there are others that are a little perplexing—the origins of things like shuttlecocks, birdies, and hat tricks are not as clear. Here is a list of some whacky sports terms and the people they are actually named for.

- Zamboni: Ice resurfacing machine inventor Frank Zamboni
- Ryder Cup: British seed merchant Samuel Ryder
- Pesky's Pole (the right field foul pole at Fenway Park): Red Sox shortstop Johnny Pesky
- Axel: Norwegian figure skater Axel Paulsen
- Heisman Trophy: College football coach John Heisman

The **Biellmann spin** is a figure skating move where the skater lifts one leg back up over his or her head while spinning, creating a teardrop shape with the body. In the 1970s, Swiss skater Denise Biellmann popularized the maneuver and gave the technique her name.

∘°ₒ°∘

The **Fosbury Flop** is a style of approaching and landing a high jump. The technique was first used by American Dick Fosbury in 1965, who later used it to win an Olympic gold medal in Mexico City in 1968.

∘°ₒ°∘

A **triple-double** occurs when a basketball player accumulates double digits in three of five statistical categories in a game: points, rebounds, assists, steals, or blocked shots. Oscar Robertson is the only player to average a triple-double for an entire season (1961–1962).

∘°ₒ°∘

Baseball's **Triple Crown** is earned when a player leads the American or National League in batting average, home runs, and runs batted in (RBIs) over a regular season. Rogers Hornsby, a two-time Triple Crown winner, had a .424 batting average in 1924. Red Sox player Carl Yastrzemski earned the Triple Crown in 1967 and held the record until 2012 when Miguel Cabrera won it playing for the Detroit Tigers.

∘°ₒ°∘

Horse racing's **Triple Crown** is earned when a horse wins the three major racing events in a given year: Kentucky Derby, Preakness, and Belmont Stakes. The last horse to accomplish this feat was Affirmed in 1978. Seattle Slew won all three races the previous year in 1977 and Secretariat achieved this feat in 1973.

SCANDALS
7 POINTS

The Cincinnati Reds "won" the infamous **1919 World Series**, which was thrown by the Chicago "Black Sox." The scandal is depicted in the movie *Eight Men Out*. One of the players embroiled in the scandal, Shoeless Joe Jackson, is the only MLB player to bat over .400 in his rookie season, batting .408 for the Indians in 1911.

∘°∘°○∘

Pete Rose holds the record for the most games played (3,562), hits (4,256), at-bats (14,053), and outs (10,328). Rose, who admitted to betting on baseball, has been passed up on Hall of Fame induction.

∘°∘°○∘

Monica Seles was the world's #1 ranked player in women's tennis in the years 1991 and 1992, at the ages of seventeen and eighteen. On April 30, 1993, Günter Parche, an avid fan of Steffi Graf, stabbed Seles in the back with a nine-inch blade on court. Seles did not return to competition for more than two years.

∘°∘°○∘

Tonya Harding, the first American woman to complete a triple axel jump in competition, found herself at the heart of a scandal when her ex-husband, Jeff Gillooly (along with two others) assaulted competitor Nancy Kerrigan with a crow bar at a practice in 1994. Seven weeks after the attack, the tape-delayed Olympic short program became one of the most watched telecasts in U.S. history. When all was said and done, Ukraine's Oksana Baiul took the gold, Kerrigan took the silver, and Harding placed 8th.

○ ° ○ ° ○ °

NBA player **Ron Artest**, who chose jersey #37 to honor the number of weeks that Michael Jackson's *Thriller* spent at #1 on the music charts, legally changed his name to Metta World Peace in 2011. Artest also served the longest suspension in NBA history (eighty-six games, nondrug related) for his role in the Pacers-Pistons brawl in November 2004.

○ ° ○ ° ○ °

Spygate, as it came to be known, refers to the 2007 New England Patriots who were disciplined by the NFL for taping the New York Jets defensive coaches from the sidelines in September 2007. Coach Bill Belichick was fined $500,000, a maximum and record amount, and the team was forced to forfeit a draft pick.

○ ° ○ ° ○ °

Causing a scandal dubbed **Bountygate**, the New Orleans Saints were accused of paying bonuses, or bounties, to players who injured opposing players as early as 2009, the year they won Super Bowl XLIV. NFL Commissioner Roger Goodell suspended head coach Sean Payton for the entire 2012 season, fined the team $500,000, and forced them to forfeit two draft picks. Linebacker Jonathan Vilma was also suspended for the entire 2012 season.

○ ° ○ ° ○ °

Eldrick "Tiger" Woods is the only individual to be named Sports Illustrated Sportsman of the Year twice, in 1996 and 2000. After he won the Masters in 1997, Tiger became one of the most successful golfers and highest paid athletes of all time. In early 2010 he admitted to infidelity with several women, and he fell to #58 on golf's world rankings by November 2011.

∘°₀°○∘

Just prior to the 2006 NFL draft, accusations of **Reggie Bush**'s family receiving gifts surfaced, in violation of NCAA policies. Following an investigation, Reggie Bush was stripped of his Heisman Trophy, and the USC Trojans received a two-season postseason ban and their wins were vacated for their 2004–2005 championship season.

∘°₀°○∘

Having survived testicular cancer that spread to his brain and lungs, **Lance Armstrong** went on to win the Tour de France seven times in a row between 1999 and 2005. His charitable foundation, Livestrong, has raised the most money of any athlete's charity. In 2012, Armstrong was found in violation of the World Anti-Doping Agency Code, which he later admitted to on *Oprah*, and was stripped of all his Tour de France titles.

∘°₀°○∘

Alex Rodriguez is the youngest player ever to hit 500 and 600 home runs. A-Rod is a three-time MVP and holds the record for most grand slams (twenty-four). In 2009, A-Rod admitted to using steroids earlier in his career and, in 2013, was suspended for the entire 2014 season.

SPORTS HALLS OF FAME

 Just as there are many sports, so are there many Halls of Fame. You can find each one at the following locations.

- Pro Football Hall of Fame: Canton, Ohio
- National Soccer Hall of Fame: Oneonta, New York
- National Baseball Hall of Fame and Museum: Cooperstown, New York
- Naismith Memorial Basketball Hall of Fame: Springfield, Massachusetts
- United States Hockey Hall of Fame: Eveleth, Minnesota
- NASCAR Hall of Fame: Charlotte, North Carolina
- America's Cup Hall of Fame: Bristol, Rhode Island
- National Wrestling Hall of Fame: Stillwater, Oklahoma
- United States Bicycling Hall of Fame: Davis, California
- World Figure Skating Museum and Hall of Fame: Colorado Springs, Colorado
- International Gymnastics Hall of Fame: Oklahoma City, Oklahoma
- International Bowling Museum and Hall of Fame: Arlington, Texas

CHAPTER 12

OLYMPICS

Do you know . . .

- Which country hosted the games when the USA boycotted in 1980?
- What individual athlete has won the most gold medals?
- What Olympian appeared in the disco dud *Can't Stop the Music* (1980)?
- Who was the only American to win a gold medal in the 1968 Winter Olympics?
- What are the only three events where male and female athletes compete head-to-head, excluding mixed events?

If you're not sure how to answer these questions, it's time to brush up on your Olympic facts! The Olympics may only come once every two years, but questions about the Olympics appear much more frequently during pub quizzes—and if it's an Olympic year, their inclusion is virtually guaranteed. The games continue to evolve while preserving traditions of the centuries-old ancient Greek games, so it can be very challenging to know so many years, athletes, nations, and records of note. Stick with the majors, and you should be fine. Know your dates and host cities, remember some of the well-known athletes. Think: Bruce Jenner, FloJo, the Dream Team, Nancy Kerrigan, Michael Phelps, and whoever the next big thing will be when the torch is lit once again.

OLYMPIC HISTORY

1 POINT

The modern Summer Olympic Games began in 1896 in **Athens, Greece**, and have been scheduled every four years since.

∘°ₒ°○∘

The Winter Olympic Games were first held in **Chamonix, France**, in 1924 and were held in the same year as the Summer Olympics until 1998.

∘°ₒ°○∘

As of 2014, the USA had won the most **Olympic medals** overall (2,681), followed by Russia/Soviet Union (1,204), Great Britain (806), Germany (782), and France (780).

∘°ₒ°○∘

The Olympics were **canceled** on three occasions: Berlin (1916) due to WWI; Tokyo, which then relocated to Helsinki (1940), and London (1944) due to WWII.

∘°ₒ°○∘

The Olympics were first televised in Berlin (1936). At these games, Adolf Hitler refused to shake the hand of **Jesse Owens**, who won four gold medals there.

In 1948, Germany and Japan were **banned** from the Olympic Games because of their actions during WWII. In 1962, South Africa was banned for apartheid, and Rhodesia/Zimbabwe was not permitted to participate in 1972 due to racism practices.

∘°ₒ°○∘

Eleven Israeli athletes and coaches, a German police officer, and five Black September terrorists were killed during the **Munich Olympics** (1972). It was the second Summer Games held in Germany since 1936 (Berlin).

∘°ₒ°○∘

The Summer Olympics have been hosted in **three American cities**: Atlanta (1996), Los Angeles (1932, 1984), and St. Louis (1904).

∘°ₒ°○∘

Montreal hosted the Summer Olympics in 1976. At these games, Polish discus thrower Danuta Rosani became the first Olympic competitor to be expelled for drugs, and Nadia Comaneci received the first perfect score of 10 for Romania in an Olympic gymnastics competition (uneven bars). The *Young and the Restless* theme song was renamed "Nadia's Theme" after her performance.

∘°ₒ°○∘

Sixty-four countries, including the USA, boycotted the **1980 Moscow Olympics** because of the Soviet Union's invasion of Afghanistan.

The Soviets would go on to win a record 197 medals, with only eighty countries participating.

∘ᵒ∘ᵒO∘

China made its first appearance in the Summer Olympics in 1984.

∘ᵒ∘ᵒO∘

London and Athens are the only cities to host the Summer games three times. London hosted in 1908, 1948, 2012; and Athens hosted in 1896, 1906, and 2004. Paris (1904 and 1924) and Los Angeles (1932 and 1984) have both hosted the Summer Olympics twice.

∘ᵒ∘ᵒO∘

Great Britain is the only country to have won at least one gold medal at every Summer Olympic Games.

∘ᵒ∘ᵒO∘

In 1988, **North Korea** boycotted the Seoul Summer Olympics after its demand to cohost the games was refused.

∘ᵒ∘ᵒO∘

Of the five continents symbolized by the **Olympic rings**, Africa is the only one never to host an Olympic Games. One ring represents North and South America. The colors of the rings represent the colors of the flags participating (Antarctica is the only continent that does not participate) in the Olympics when Baron Pierre de Coubertin, cofounder of the games, created the symbol in 1912.

∘°ₒ°O∘

St. Moritz, Switzerland (1928, 1948), **Lake Placid, United States** (1932, 1980), and **Innsbruck, Austria** (1964, 1976), have each hosted the Winter Olympics twice.

∘°ₒ°O∘

The Winter Olympics were held in 1992 in **Albertville, France**, and then were held two years later in **Lillehammer, Norway** (1994). The year 1994 was the first year that the Winter and Summer Olympics were separated by two years.

SUMMER OLYMPICS
3 POINTS

The word **marathon** comes from the Greek battlefield of Marathon. In 490 B.C., Pheidippides, a Greek soldier, was sent to Athens to spread word of the victory over the Persians. Running 42,195 meters, or 26 miles and 385 yards (.22 of a mile), he died upon arrival.

∘°ₒ°O∘

Frank Shorter is the first American to win a gold medal in the marathon. His 1972 victory sparked a jogging craze in the United States.

Ethiopia has won the most gold medals in the men's Olympic marathon (four). The country won this event in Rome (1960), Tokyo (1964), Mexico City (1968), and Sydney (2000).

Mary Lou Retton (1984), **Carly Patterson** (2004), **Nastia Liukin** (2008), and **Gabby Douglas** (2012) are the USA women who have won the coveted individual all-around gold medal in the Olympics. Dominique Dawes is the first black woman of any nationality to win an Olympic gold in gymnastics.

Badminton, **equestrian**, and **sailing** are the only three events where male and female athletes compete head-to-head, excluding mixed events.

Rhythmic gymnastics is a team or individual event where competitors manipulate a ball, a hoop, clubs, ribbon, or rope; or perform a free routine (no apparatus).

The **biathlon**, whose term originates from Norway's military training practices, made its official Olympic debut in 1960 (Squaw Valley, USA). The event combines cross-country skiing and rifle shooting.

The **triathlon** debuted in the Olympics in 2000 (Sydney). The race covers roughly 32 miles, with a 0.93-mile swim, a 25-mile cycle, and a 6.2-mile run.

○ °○° ○ ○

The **pentathlon** originates from the Ancient Olympics. Its events then included the long jump, javelin, discus, foot race, and wrestling. The modern event is comprised of an equestrian competition, épée fencing matches, pistol shooting, a 300-meter freestyle swim, and a 4,000-meter cross-country run.

JIM THORPE

At the 1912 Summer Olympics in Stockholm, USA athlete Jim Thorpe won the gold medal for the pentathlon and the decathlon. However, he was stripped of both medals when it was discovered that he had played two seasons of semiprofessional baseball before competing at the Olympics. At the time the games had strict rules about amateurism that stated that athletes could not have been paid for athletic events before competing in an Olympics. He went on to play professional baseball and football. In 1983, thirty years after his death, and after serious lobbying, the Executive Board of the International Olympic Committee agreed to reinstate Thorpe's two medals.

WINTER OLYMPICS
5 POINTS

In the **Miracle on Ice**, Mike Eruzione scored the go-ahead goal against the Soviet Union in the 1980 Olympic hockey semifinal game. Al Michaels called the game, exclaiming, "Do you believe in miracles? Yes!" The USA went on to beat Finland in the final to win the gold medal.

○ °○° ○

Soviet goalie **Vladislav Tretiak** is the only male athlete to have won one silver and three gold medals in ice hockey.

○ °○° ○

Norway has won the most gold (118), silver (111), bronze (100), and total medals (329) in the Winter Olympics. The USA has the second most medals with 281.

○ °○° ○

Olympic **ski jumping** saw its debut in Norway. Since the 1992 games, the height of the jump has remained consistent at 394 feet. A panel of five judges rate the athletes' form on a scale from 0 to 20, factoring in distance. A perfect score is 60.

Hockey player **Sidney Crosby** scored the winning goal for Canada in the 2010 Olympics. He also scored in Canada's 3–0 victory over Sweden in the 2014 Gold Medal game.

Julia Mancuso is the first American skier to win Alpine medals at three consecutive Olympics.

Shani Davis, a speed skater, became the first African American athlete to win an individual gold medal at the Winter Olympics when he won in 2006 in Turin, Italy. Vonetta Flowers was the first African American to win Winter Olympic gold, for bobsled, in 2002 (Salt Lake City, Utah).

With eight, **Apolo Ohno** has the most Winter Olympic medals among American athletes.

Two-time Olympic gold medal winner in snowboard cross **Seth Wescott** resides near Sugarloaf Mountain in Maine, where he owns a restaurant called The Rack.

Figure skater **Peggy Fleming** was the only American to win a gold medal at the 1968 Winter Olympics in Grenoble, France. Dorothy Hamill (1976), Kristi Yamaguchi (1992), Tara Lipinski (1998), and Sarah Hughes (2000) have since won gold in women's singles figure skating.

NOTED OLYMPIANS
7 POINTS

A.C. Gilbert, the inventor of the Erector set (1913), won an Olympic gold medal in 1908 in the pole vault competition at the London games.

∘°o°O∘

Dr. Benjamin Spock (author of *Baby and Child Care*, 1946) won an Olympic gold medal. While attending Yale, he was a member of the school's rowing team, which competed in the 1924 Paris Olympics and won gold.

∘°o°O∘

Alice Coachman was the first African American female athlete to win a gold medal in the Summer Olympics. She won in 1948 in London for the high jump.

∘°o°O∘

United Kingdom runners **Harold Abrahams** (gold, 100 meters) and **Eric Liddell** (gold, 400 meters) were portrayed in the film *Chariots of Fire* (1981), which depicts their triumph in the Paris Olympics (1924).

○ ○ ○ ○ ○

Joe Frazier was the first American boxer to win both the Olympic gold medal (1964, Tokyo) and the professional world title in the heavyweight division. Sugar Ray Leonard and brothers Leon and Michael Spinks all won gold medals in 1976 in Montreal. Michael went on to become light heavyweight and heavyweight boxing champion of the world.

○ ○ ○ ○ ○

Bruce Jenner won the decathlon in Montreal (1976). Following Olympic fame, Jenner appeared on the TV series *Chips* and the disco dud *Can't Stop the Music* (1980). The film won the first Golden Raspberry Award for Worst Picture. These days Bruce Jenner is better known for his adopted family—the Kardashians.

○ ○ ○ ○ ○

Greg Louganis swept the diving events in consecutive Olympic Games (1984 and 1988). Louganis received the James E. Sullivan Award in 1984 for outstanding amateur athlete in the United States.

○ ○ ○ ○ ○

Mitch Gaylord won four medals at the 1984 Olympics, went on to star in the movie *American Anthem* (1986), and acted as Chris O'Donnell's stunt double in *Batman Forever* (1995).

Steffi Graf is the only tennis player to achieve the Golden Slam—capturing all four Grand Slam singles titles and the Olympic Gold medal in the same year, 1988. In 2001, Graf married former #1 ranked tennis star Andre Agassi.

∘O∘O∘O∘

Grace Kelly's brother, **John B. Kelly Jr.**, won a bronze medal in single scull rowing in 1956. Her son, Albert II, Prince of Monaco, competed in bobsled in every Winter Olympics from Calgary to Salt Lake City.

∘O∘O∘O∘

Track star **Marion Jones** won five medals at the 2000 Summer Olympics in Sydney but has since agreed to forfeit all of them after admitting to taking performance-enhancing drugs. Sprinter **Ben Johnson** of Canada won two bronze medals in 1984 (Los Angeles) and a gold in 1988 (Seoul) but was later disqualified for doping.

∘O∘O∘O∘

Jackie Joyner-Kersee won three gold, one silver, and two bronze medals and appeared in four different Olympic games (1984–1996), competing in the long jump and women's heptathlon.

∘O∘O∘O∘

Clara Hughes is the fourth person in history to win a medal in both the Summer and Winter Olympics. As a cyclist and speed skater, Hughes won medals in 1996 (Atlanta) and 2002 (Salt Lake City).

Usain Bolt (Jamaica) is the first man to win six Olympic gold medals in sprinting. The last man to win three sprinting gold medals in one Olympics is Carl Lewis (1984). Carl Lewis would be drafted by both the Dallas Cowboys and Chicago Bulls in 1984.

₀ ᵒOₒᵒOₒ ₒ

Michael Phelps is the most decorated Olympian of all time with twenty-two medals, the most gold medals (eighteen), and the most first place finishes at any one Olympic games.

OLYMPICS SPORT DEBUTS

Over the years, many Olympic sports have come and gone. Check out some interesting debuts here:

- First women's event (Tennis): 1900 (Paris)
- Basketball: 1936 (Berlin)
- Canoeing and kayaking: 1936 (Berlin)
- Synchronized swimming: 1984 (Los Angeles)
- Table tennis: 1988 (Seoul)
- Badminton: 1992 (Barcelona)
- Beach volleyball: 1996 (Atlanta)
- Snowboarding: 1998 (Nagano)
- Trampolining: 2000 (Sydney)
- Ski cross: 2010 (Vancouver)
- Figure skating team event: (2014) Sochi

BUSINESS

Do you know . . .

- Who was the first to use an assembly line in auto manufacturing?
- Who is the richest American?
- Which U.S. company is the largest private employer in the world?
- Where was the first Dunkin' Donuts located?
- Which company takes its name from the first mate in Herman Melville's classic *Moby-Dick*?

Did any of these answers pop into your head? If not, you're in good company. The good news is that the Business category is not as common as some of the other pop culture categories, but if you're at a good trivia night, the odds are it will come up every once in a while. Unless your pub quiz is on Wall Street, the Business category is probably not going to involve too deep of a dive into the Dow Jones, but this chapter will give you a good head start with info on which companies own which other companies, the history of business (you should have paid better attention in the tenth grade), and where to walk the line when business and pop culture intersect.

TECH TALK
(1 POINT)

Hewlett-Packard was started in a garage in Palo Alto, and its first big customer was Walt Disney, who bought eight oscillators for the surround sound of *Fantasia* (1940).

○ ○ ○ ○ ○

On June 26, 1974, the first product with a bar code scanned at a checkout counter was a ten-pack of **Wrigley's Juicy Fruit** chewing gum.

○ ○ ○ ○ ○

Video Game Hall of Fame inductee Nolan Bushnell, the inventor of Atari, founded **Chuck E. Cheese** in 1977. It was the first family restaurant to integrate food, animated entertainment, and video games. Bushnell was named one of *Newsweek*'s "50 Men Who Changed America."

○ ○ ○ ○ ○

The Guinness Book of Records credits American businessman **Mark Cuban** with the "largest single e-commerce transaction," for paying $40 million for his Gulfstream V jet in 1999. That same year, Cuban sold Broadcast.com to Yahoo! for $5.9 billion in Yahoo! stock. In 2000, he went on to buy the Dallas Mavericks for $285 million.

○ ○ ○ ○ ○

Founded by Jeff Bezos in 1994, **Amazon.com** was originally launched as Cadabra.com. Headquartered in Seattle, Amazon.com is the world's largest online retailer.

∘°∘°O∘

Shawn Fanning and Sean Parker founded **Napster** in 1999 while Fanning was attending Northeastern University.

∘°∘°O∘

Kintaro Hattori founded **Seiko** in 1881.

∘°∘°O∘

Edwin Land invented the Land Camera, later known as **Polaroid**, in 1948.

∘°∘°O∘

Bell Telephone was founded in Boston in 1877.

∘°∘°O∘

Motorola devised a management program called Six Sigma, which was formulated by Bill Smith in 1986.

∘°∘°O∘

BlackBerry, introduced in 1999, was developed by the Canadian company Research in Motion.

∘°∘°○∘

French-born programmer Pierre Omidyar founded **eBay**, which was named as a tongue-in-cheek tribute to the Ebola virus. The first item sold on eBay was a broken laser pointer for $14.83 in 1995.

∘°∘°○∘

Larry Ellison founded **Oracle**, the second largest software maker after Microsoft, in 1977. Today Ellison is the third richest man in America after Bill Gates (Microsoft) and Warren Buffett (Berkshire Hathaway). Ellison's Oracle Team USA won the 2010 and 2013 America's Cup.

∘°∘°○∘

Ronald Wayne, Steve Jobs, and Steve Wozniak founded **Apple** in Cupertino, California, in 1976. As a retailer, Apple does the most sales per square foot ($4,500) at its stores. Tiffany's is second at $3,000 per square foot.

∘°∘°○∘

According to *The Guinness Book of World Records*, **Sex.com** is the world's most expensive domain name, purchased for $13 million in 2010.

RETAIL

3 POINTS

Abercrombie & Fitch was a sporting goods business that went bankrupt in 1977. It was resurrected as a clothing retailer after its brand name was sold in 1988.

∘°ₒ°O∘

Headquartered in Freeport, Maine, **L.L. Bean** got its start with the invention of a rubber-soled fishing boot in Greenwood, Maine, in 1912.

∘°ₒ°O∘

Brothers Henry and Helal Hassenfeld originally established **Hasbro**, a toy and board-game company, in 1923 as a textile remnant company.

∘°ₒ°O∘

Based in Boulder, Colorado, **Spyder** is the official outerwear supplier to the U.S. Alpine Ski Team.

∘°ₒ°O∘

In 1987, **Owens Corning**, a maker of fiberglass insulation, became the first company to trademark a color, pink.

∘°ₒ°O∘

Many celebrities have started successful clothing lines, including the following:

- **Phat Farm**—Russell Simmons of Run-D.M.C.
- **G-Unit Clothing Company**—50 Cent
- **Rocawear**—Jay-Z
- **Dualstar** and **The Row**—Mary-Kate and Ashley Olsen
- **L.A.M.B.**—Gwen Stefani
- **Atticus Clothing**—Mark Hoppus and Tom DeLonge of Blink-182
- **Clandestine**—Pete Wentz of Fall Out Boy

○ ᵒＯᵒＯ ○

Dassler Brothers' running shoes gained popularity after Jesse Owens wore them in the 1936 Summer Olympics. In 1948, the Dassler brothers' partnership dissolved. Adi Dassler went on to create **Adidas**, and his brother, Rudi, started **Puma**.

○ ᵒＯᵒＯ ○

Joseph Foster founded **Reebok** in 1892. The company, named after a species of South African antelope, makes all of the uniforms for the NFL and NHL.

○ ᵒＯᵒＯ ○

Phil Knight and Bill Bowerman started **Nike** in 1964. Bowerman was Knight's former track coach at the University of Oregon.

Roy Raymond first opened **Victoria's Secret** in San Francisco in 1977. Raymond later committed suicide in 1993 at the age of forty-seven by jumping off the Golden Gate Bridge.

Founded in 1818, **Brooks Brothers**, which provided the suits worn by Teddy Roosevelt and Woodrow Wilson at their presidential inaugurations, is the oldest surviving men's clothier in the United States. F. Scott Fitzgerald and Ernest Hemingway both mentioned the company in their books.

In 1871, one year after trademark laws were passed, **Fruit of the Loom** received the first trademark in the textile industry.

In 1956, the first enclosed, **climate-controlled mall** opened in Edina, Minnesota.

Harley-Davidson's factory is on the outskirts of Milwaukee, Wisconsin.

Nike's advertising slogan, "Just Do It," was inspired by the last words of convicted murderer Gary Gilmore ("Let's do it"), who was executed by a firing squad in 1977. The Police's song "Bring on the Night" speculated on Gary Gilmore's possible feelings.

COMPANY NAMES SPELLED OUT

Ever wonder what all those abbreviated company names really stand for? Wonder no longer!

- 3M: Minnesota Mining and Manufacturing Company
- SUN Microsystems: Stanford University Network
- Xerox: Greek for "dry writing"
- HMO: Health Maintenance Organization
- QVC: Quality, Value, Convenience
- Volvo: Latin for "I roll"
- SAAB: Swedish for "Swedish Airplane Limited"
- BMW: Bavarian Motor Works
- IBM: International Business Machines
- CVS: Customer Value Stores

≡ BIG BUSINESS ≡
5 POINTS

Henry Ford introduced the eight-hour, five-day work week to Americans.

∘°○°○∘

Henry Ford's **Model T** was made for only nineteen years, selling for $825 in 1908 and $360 in 1927.

₀O₀°O₀

Ransom E. Olds was the first to use the assembly line in the auto industry and has two car companies named for him: Oldsmobile and REO Motor Car Company.

₀O₀°O₀

In 1870, John Rockefeller founded **Standard Oil** in Ohio. The company became the largest oil refinery in the world. In 1911, the U.S. Supreme Court ruled that it was an illegal monopoly and ordered it to break up into ninety different companies. Exxon, Amoco, Mobil, and Chevron were all created as a result of this order.

₀O₀°O₀

Oil company owner **Leon Hess** bought out his fellow co-owners of the New York Titans in 1963 and renamed the team the Jets, changing the team's colors in the process.

₀O₀°O₀

On the 2013 *Fortune* Global 500 list, of "the 500 largest corporations in the world" **Walmart** is the only entry in the Top 5 that is not in the energy/oil industry. Walmart is the largest private employer in the world and the second-largest employer overall, trailing only the Chinese Army.

○°○°○°○○

The oil company **Saudi Aramco**, located in Saudi Arabia, is estimated to be valued at $10 trillion, making it the most valuable company in the world.

○°○°○°○○

Tesla produced a 2013 car that *Consumer Reports* gave a score of 99 out of 100—higher than any other car ever tested.

○°○°○°○○

Approximately half of all ***Fortune* 500** companies are headquartered in Delaware.

○°○°○°○○

General Electric has been tracked on the Dow longer than any other company. In 1998, the 106-year-old company became the first in the United States to top $300 billion in market value.

○°○°○°○○

Target started in 1902 as the Dayton Dry Goods Company. The first Target store opened in Minnesota in 1962.

○°○°○°○○

J. Willard Marriott started the **Marriott Corporation** in Virginia in 1927. Originally, the company was a food service company called Hot Shoppes; it kept this name until 1967. The last Hot Shoppes restaurant, located in Maryland, closed in December 1999. Former state governor and U.S. presidential candidate Willard Mitt Romney was named after the Marriott founder.

○°○°○○

Colt was the first American manufacturer to establish a foreign branch, opening a factory in London to supply the British with weapons during the Crimean War.

○°○°○○

In 1997, **Toyota Corolla** became the bestselling car brand of all time.

○°○°○○

Porsche designed the Volkswagen Beetle, the Tiger tank, and a "people's car" for Adolf Hitler. Porsche, started by Ferdinand Porsche, used the coat of arms of Stuttgart, Germany, as its logo.

○°○°○○

Volkswagen opened a Pennsylvania plant in 1978, becoming the first foreign company to open a factory in the United States.

FOOD AND BEVERAGES

7 POINTS

Altoids, "The Original Celebrated Curiously Strong Mints," were introduced in England in 1780 during the reign of King George III.

○°○°○○

Civil War Colonel John Pemberton invented **Coca-Cola** in 1886. Pemberton, who became addicted to morphine after being wounded, was on a quest for a substitute. The Coca-Cola trademark, written in the Spencerian script by the bookkeeper, Frank Robinson, was registered in 1893.

○°○°○○

Red Bull, the most popular energy drink in the world, was founded in Salzburg, Austria, in 1984.

○°○°○○

Guinness Brewery, a.k.a. St. James's Gate Brewery, holds a record 9,000 year lease on its property.

○°○°○○

Bass Ale is England's first registered trademark and is also, arguably, the world's first trademark. It was registered in 1875.

Peet's Coffee & Tea was founded in 1966 in San Francisco. **Starbucks**, a spinoff of Peet's, was founded in Seattle in 1971. Starbucks took its name from the first mate in Herman Melville's classic *Moby-Dick*.

Vodka outsold whiskey in the United States for the first time in 1972.

Kraft Foods Group Inc. is the largest candy, food, and beverage company headquartered in the United States. It is the second largest in the world after Nestlé (Switzerland).

The International Balloon Race at the Indianapolis Speedway inspired **Wonder Bread**'s familiar red, white, blue, and yellow packaging.

Hooters was founded in Atlanta in 1983. The staff uniforms are said to be based on those of the women's track team at Clemson University. The label colors of **Campbell's soup** products were inspired by the Cornell University football team. A company executive suggested the colors after attending a game in 1898.

TGI Fridays is credited with inventing the Loaded Potato Skins in 1974.

Founded in 1921, **White Castle** is credited as being the first fast food chain. The burgers cost five cents in the 1940s. In 2014, *Time* called the White Castle slider "the most influential burger of all time."

Tom Monaghan, a Catholic philanthropist, founded **Domino's Pizza** in Ann Arbor, Michigan, in 1960.

Introduced in 1967, **Pringles** was originally called Pringles Newfangled Potato Chips.

Black Jack, brought to the United States by Mexican President Santa Anna, became the first flavored gum in the United States. It tasted like licorice and was also the first gum to be offered in sticks.

Trident invented the first sugarless gum in 1960.

Toblerone received a patent in 1909 to keep other chocolates from copying its signature triangle shape.

Yale Law School graduates Tim and Nina Zagat founded the **Zagat Survey** in New York City in 1979. It was sold to Google for $151 million in 2011.

India is the largest producer of mangoes and bananas in the world; **Brazil** is the largest producer of coffee; and **Mexico** is the largest producer of avocados, lemons, and limes.

New York is the largest producer of yogurt and the second largest producer of maple syrup in the United States after Vermont.

The first **Dunkin' Donuts** was established in 1950 in Quincy, Massachusetts.

Snickers is the bestselling candy bar of all time. It first debuted in 1930 and was named for a horse that the Mars family owned.

$_{\circ}{}^{O}{}_{O}{}^{\circ}O{}_{\circ}$

M&M stands for the founders of the candy company Mars, Inc.: Mars and Murrie.

COMPANY MASCOTS

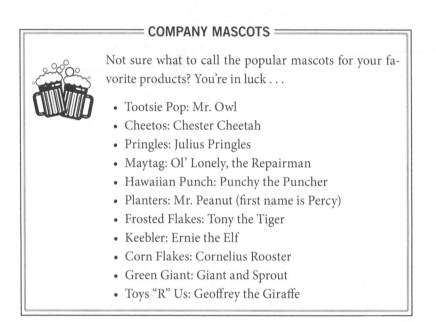

Not sure what to call the popular mascots for your favorite products? You're in luck . . .

- Tootsie Pop: Mr. Owl
- Cheetos: Chester Cheetah
- Pringles: Julius Pringles
- Maytag: Ol' Lonely, the Repairman
- Hawaiian Punch: Punchy the Puncher
- Planters: Mr. Peanut (first name is Percy)
- Frosted Flakes: Tony the Tiger
- Keebler: Ernie the Elf
- Corn Flakes: Cornelius Rooster
- Green Giant: Giant and Sprout
- Toys "R" Us: Geoffrey the Giraffe

CHAPTER 14

CURRENCY

Do you know . . .

- In colonial days, how much money was two bits?
- The nickname for Canada's one dollar coin?
- What other countries use U.S. dollars?
- What company released the first credit card?
- What is the most common day for a bank robbery?

If you knew the answers to all of these questions, congratulations! If not, remember that money is continually changing, encompassing every part of the world, and is often affected by politics, which means the Currency category could be a bit of a challenge. Fortunately, the facts in this chapter will give you the info you need to win. Commonly, trivia masters will ask who appears on coins, bills, and notes, so memorize American money, and try to also make your way around the world with the euro and some of the other well-known currencies. You'll also come across currency questions masquerading as other categories. For example, if you're asked who appears on the $10 bill (Alexander Hamilton), the odds are that the trivia master will find a way to work in the duel with Aaron Burr that ended Hamilton's life. If this tricky sort of questioning doesn't get you hooked on pub quizzes, well . . . you can always join a dart league instead.

AMERICAN MONEY
1 POINT

In colonial days in the United States, when the **Spanish milled dollar** was a common unit of currency, two bits was worth twenty-five cents.

○°○°○○

The back of an older $10 bill is the only American paper currency that contains the picture of an automobile, a 1926 **Hupmobile**.

○°○°○○

On coins minted in the United States, cities represented by the **mint marks** D, P, S, and O stand for Denver, Philadelphia, San Francisco, and New Orleans. Fort Worth is the only location other than Washington, D.C., that prints paper U.S. currency.

○°○°○○

More **$1 bills** are printed annually in the United States than any other denomination. The $20 bill ranks second.

○°○°○○

The **U.S. gold depository** is located in Fort Knox, Kentucky. The U.S. silver depository is located in West Point, New York.

○°○°○○

The only **nonpresidents** to be commemorated on the front of U.S. coins or paper currency are:
- Susan B. Anthony—$1 coin
- Sacagawea and infant son—$1 coin
- Alexander Hamilton—$10 bill
- Benjamin Franklin—$100 bill
- Salmon P. Chase—$10,000 bill

。ᵒₒ°○。

The **Abraham Lincoln penny** is the only U.S. coin in which the portrait faces to the right.

。ᵒₒ°○。

Since 1982, at least 97.5 percent of a **Lincoln cent** has been made from zinc, with 2.5 percent copper plating.

。ᵒₒ°○。

According to the **U.S. Bureau of Engraving and Printing**, U.S. currency is printed on paper made up of 75 percent cotton and 25 percent linen.

。ᵒₒ°○。

The $20 1933 **Double Eagle gold coin** holds the record for the second-highest price paid at auction for a single U.S. coin, selling for $7.59 million. The highest price paid for a coin was $10 million, which was paid out for the 1794 Flowing Hair Dollar.

∘°ₒ°O∘

T-bills, notes, and bonds have different **durations**, the amount of time it takes for repayment. The duration for T-bills is less than a year, notes is up to 10 years, and bonds is longer than 10 years.

∘°ₒ°O∘

Last printed in 1934, **high denomination bills** were taken out of circulation in 1969. Some still exist today but are very rare. They have the following portraits:
- $500—William McKinley
- $1,000—Grover Cleveland
- $5,000—James Madison
- $10,000—Salmon P. Chase
- $100,000—Woodrow Wilson

∘°ₒ°O∘

If you were to lay out a mile of **pennies**, you would have $844.80.

WORLD CURRENCY
3 POINTS

Israel was the first country to picture **Albert Einstein** on its banknotes.

The nickname of the Canadian $1 coin is a **loonie**, named for their National Bird, the loon.

The **Jack Nicklaus** is the only living person to be featured on a Scottish banknote.

The **pound sterling**, or pound, is the official currency of the United Kingdom. It is the fourth most traded currency in the foreign exchange market after the U.S. dollar, the euro, and the Japanese yen.

The **euro** was adopted in December 1995 and was introduced to world markets in 1999, with coins and banknotes entering circulation in 2002.

There are ten members of the **European Union** that do not use the euro: Bulgaria, Czech Republic, Denmark, Croatia, Lithuania, Hungary, Poland, Romania, Sweden, and the United Kingdom.

Iceland's top ranking on the World Happiness Report was endangered when the country went bankrupt during its 2008 financial crisis.

CURRENCY NAMES

You know the name of the currency that you spend every day, but do you know what your counterparts are spending around the world? Here are the names of some international currency to keep you in the game.

- Brazil: real
- Guatemala: quetzal
- Vietnam: dong
- Turkey, Cyprus, Malta, Lebanon: lira
- Iceland and Sweden: krona
- Denmark: krone
- Venezuela: bolivar
- Poland: zloty
- Angola: kwanza
- Costa Rica and El Salvador: colón
- Argentina, Chile, Colombia, Cuba, Dominican Republic, Mexico, Philippines, Uruguay: peso
- Panama: balboa

Taiwan features baseball on their currency because its Little League teams have won eleven Little League World Series Championships. Other countries with sports on their currency include Scotland (golf), Canada (hockey), and Greece (discus).

₀°₀°O₀

Eva Perón replaced the image of Julio Argentino Roca on a currency note in Argentina.

₀°₀°O₀

China was the first country to use paper money.

∘°₀°○∘

East Timor, Ecuador, El Salvador, Micronesia, Palau, and Zimbabwe use the **U.S. dollar** for currency.

∘°₀°○∘

The **dinar** is the currency of Algeria, Bahrain, Iraq, Jordan, Kuwait, Libya, Macedonia, Serbia, and Tunisia. The 100 Serbian dinar note depicts Nikola Tesla.

═══ MARKETS ═══
5 POINTS

Since 1986, the *Economist* has published an annual feature measuring **purchasing power** parity by listing the price in U.S. dollars to buy a McDonald's Big Mac in countries around the world.

∘°₀°○∘

The oldest currency to be replaced by the euro was the **Greek drachma**, which was used as a form of currency as early as 1100 B.C.

∘°₀°○∘

Diners Club formed in 1950 and was the first independent credit card company in the world.

In the late 1970s, **Citibank** was the first bank to establish a network of automated teller machines (ATMs).

Belgium, The Netherlands, and Luxembourg formed an economic union called **Benelux** in 1958.

Luxembourg has the highest gross domestic product in the world.

Wampum are white and mauve beads formerly used by U.S. Native Americans as money or ornaments.

Bitcoin is a digital currency introduced in 2009. A process called "mining" creates bitcoins, which can be exchanged for goods and services using wallet software.

China is the world's largest exporter, with exports estimated at $2.057 trillion in 2013. China is followed by the United States ($1.564 trillion), Germany ($1.46 trillion), and Japan ($7.739 billion).

MO' MONEY, MO' PROBLEMS
7 POINTS

Not counting $1 coins, if each U.S. president is worth one of each coin or bill on which he appears, the total value of **Mount Rushmore** is $8.31.

∘°₀°O∘

Using only pennies, nickels, dimes, and quarters, there are 242 ways to make **change for a dollar**.

∘°₀°O∘

$1.19 is the highest amount of money you can have in change without having change for a dollar, using the smallest number of coins: 3 quarters, 4 dimes, and 4 pennies.

∘°₀°O∘

In 1921, **Charles Ponzi** duped thousands of New England residents into investing in fraudulent postage stamp speculation, raking in millions of dollars.

∘°₀°O∘

On December 11, 2008, New York investor **Bernie Madoff** was arrested for running a Ponzi scheme that defrauded investors out of an estimated $18 billion, the largest financial fraud in U.S. history. He pled guilty to eleven federal felonies and is currently serving a 150-year sentence. His son Peter was sentenced to ten years in prison, and another son, Mark, committed suicide exactly two years after the date of his father's arrest.

○ °○° ○° ○ ○

Leona Helmsley was an American businesswoman who was nick-named the "Queen of Mean" and "Queen of the Palace Hotel." In 1989, she was convicted of federal income tax evasion and sentenced to sixteen years in prison, of which she served only nineteen months. She died in 2007, and in her will left a $12 million trust for her dog.

○ °○° ○° ○ ○

In casinos, $50 bills are known as **frogs** and are considered by many to be bad luck.

○ °○° ○° ○ ○

Created under the Banking Act of 1933, the letters in **FDIC** stand for Federal Deposit Insurance Corporation.

○ °○° ○° ○ ○

TARP stands for Troubled Asset Relief Program, and it includes money given to the banks by the U.S. federal government in the $700 billion financial bailout plan of 2008.

○ °○° ○° ○ ○

A theft called the **Lufthansa heist** occurred at JFK International Airport on December 11, 1978. An estimated $5 million in cash and $875,000 in jewelry were stolen, making it the largest cash robbery on U.S. soil. The heist is a central theme in the movie *GoodFellas* (1990).

○°○°○○

On Thanksgiving eve in 1971, **D.B. Cooper** hijacked a 727 jet that was scheduled to fly from Portland to Seattle. He demanded $200,000, four parachutes, and a refuel truck. The plane took off with Cooper and the crew. Cooper jumped out somewhere over Washington state. He has never been found.

○°○°○○

Most bank robberies take place on **Fridays**.

E PLURIBUS UNUM

E pluribus unum translates from Latin to mean "Out of many, one" and can be found written on most U.S. currency. A $3 coin issued during the American Revolution had a different motto, *Exitus in dubio est* ("The outcome is in doubt"), but thankfully a committee consisting of John Adams, Benjamin Franklin, and Thomas Jefferson suggested the more optimistic motto we know and love today. *E pluribus unum* first appeared on the Great Seal of the United States in 1782, and on currency in 1902.

CHAPTER 15

VIDEO GAMES AND TOYS

Do you know . . .

- Which video game was originally called *Jumpman*?
- What is the bestselling board game of all time?
- What is the first toy advertised on TV?
- Which most-popular gift in 1984 was commemorated with a U.S. postage stamp in 1999?
- What toy is based on a weapon once used by Filipino hunters?

And the answers are . . . found throughout this chapter! This may seem like a little-used category, but during a pub quiz you'll encounter questions on video games and toys as offshoots of sports or business questions, or you may come across them in their own category. Be prepared! Video games may only be a few decades old, but we've come a long way since Pong, so it's a ripe category. Know about the biggies: *Mario*, *Zelda*, *Warcraft*, *Halo*, and *The Sims*. As for toys, classic board games and novelty toys are a good place to focus, so memorize the weapons in Clue and the properties in Monopoly, and know a thing or two about Slinky, Frisbee, and Furby. What follows are some good facts you should have in your arsenal of information.

═══ VIDEO GAMES ═══
1 POINT

Pac-Man, developed by Namco, was first released in 1980. The names of the four ghosts in *Pac-Man* are Inky, Blinky, Pinky, and Clyde. Cherry is the first fruit to appear in the *Pac-Man* maze.

∘°ₒ°O∘

In 1981, ***Donkey Kong/Super Mario Bros.*** was originally named *Jumpman* after the hero who attempts to rescue Pauline. Princess Toadstool, a.k.a. Princess Peach, is the name of the princess of Mushroom Kingdom who spends most of her time waiting to be rescued by brothers Mario and Luigi.

∘°ₒ°O∘

The original **Nintendo Entertainment System** came with the games *Gyromite*, *Duck Hunt*, and *Super Mario Bros. Hogan's Alley* (1984), one of the first games to use a light gun, was modeled after and named for the FBI drill where shooters identify and fire at the bad guys and not the innocent bystanders.

∘°ₒ°O∘

Created by the Japanese company Taito in 1978, ***Space Invaders*** is one of the earliest shooting games.

∘°ₒ°O∘

Alexey Pajitnov, a worker for the Soviet Academy of Sciences, created *Tetris* in 1984. In 2010, *Tetris* became the most downloaded game of all time. Including Game Boy, Nintendo, and mobile phone versions, *Tetris* has sold more than 140 million copies. The next bestselling video games, based on copies sold, are:

- *Wii Sports* (2006)
- *Minecraft* (2009)
- *Super Mario Bros.* (1985)
- *Mario Kart Wii* (2008)
- *Grand Theft Auto V* (2013)

∘°ₒ°O∘

Wolfenstein 3D (1992), a Nazi-hunting video game, helped popularize the "first-person shooter" perspective.

∘°ₒ°O∘

Halo is a multibillion-dollar first-person shooter, sci-fi video game franchise that debuted in 2001. *Halo* holds five Guinness World Records, including bestselling game on the Xbox.

∘°ₒ°O∘

Dr. Gordon Freeman is the protagonist in **Half-Life** (1998).

∘°ₒ°O∘

Doom, a groundbreaking first-person shooter video game released in 1993, uses the BFG9000 as the primary weapon. The game inspired four sequels and a 2005 film.

Swedish programmer Markus "Notch" Persson created **Minecraft** in 2009. In this game, players build structures with textured cubes. *Minecraft* received five awards from the 2011 Game Developers Conference.

Guitar Hero, first released in 2005, is claimed by its parent company to be the first single video game title to exceed $1 billion in sales.

═══ GAMES ═══
3 POINTS

In **Clue**, Mr. Boddy could have been killed with a knife, revolver, rope, candlestick, lead pipe, or wrench by Colonel Mustard, Professor Plum, Miss Scarlet, Mrs. Peacock, Mr. Green, or Mrs. White in the ballroom, billiard room, conservatory, dining room, kitchen, lounge, library, study, or hall.

Eleanor Abbott invented **Candy Land** while she recovered from Polio in 1949.

Seventeenth-century English poet Sir John A. Suckling invented **Cribbage**.

Canadians John and Chris Haney and Scott Abbott invented **Trivial Pursuit** in 1979. The game reached its peak of popularity in 1984 when twenty million games were sold.

In 1938, Alfred Butts invented Criss-Crosswords, which became known as **Scrabble** in 1948. It's called a "Bingo" when a player uses all seven tiles at once in Scrabble.

Parcheesi is known as the "Royal Game of India."

Cavity Sam is the name of the patient in the game ***Operation***. The breadbasket, a.k.a. stomach, is the highest-scoring area on which to operate.

Whist, a forerunner of bridge, originated the term "grand slam," which indicated winning all thirteen tricks in a hand.

∘°∘°O∘

The Landlord's Game, patented in 1904 by a Quaker named Elizabeth Magie, was the inspiration for **Monopoly**, the bestselling board game of all time.

∘°∘°O∘

Reversi is a strategy game where players take turns placing a black-and-white disc on a green board. This game is also known as Othello, which is a name based on the play by Shakespeare.

∘°∘°O∘

Cards Against Humanity was created in Illinois by a group of Highland Park High School alumni for a New Year's Eve party. The first expansion game version was released in November 2011 and sold out in three days.

∘°∘°O∘

Brett Carrow and Sam Hennemann set the Guinness World Record for most consecutive hours playing a board game. They played **Strat-O-Matic**, a baseball simulation game, for more than sixty-one straight hours.

THE BUSINESS
OF FUN
5 POINTS

Nintendo was founded in 1889 as the **Marufuku Company**, a distributor of playing cards. The name was changed in 1951. Nintendo is a majority owner of the Seattle Mariners and also owns Pokémon (1996).

∘°∘°∘∘

Midway Games released their first hit, *Space Invaders*, in 1987 and later released classic arcade games like *Spy Hunter*, *Mortal Kombat*, *and Ms. Pac-Man*. In 2009, Midway filed for bankruptcy.

∘°∘°∘∘

Matchbox was started in the United Kingdom in 1953. Their die-cast car toys were sold in boxes of a similar size to matches, hence the name Matchbox.

∘°∘°∘∘

American toy maker Mattel introduced **Hot Wheels** in 1968. As a competitor to Matchbox, Hot Wheels "tricked out" their toy vehicles and revolutionized the toy car industry. In 1997, Mattel bought Tyco Toys, then the parent company of Matchbox. Competition over.

TEDDY BEAR

In November 1902, Theodore (Teddy) Roosevelt traveled to Mississippi to resolve a border dispute with Louisiana. During his free time, the president went on a bear hunting expedition and came upon a young wounded bear and ordered a mercy killing. The event inspired a story and cartoon by Clifford Berryman in the *Washington Post*. The incident inspired Morris Michtom to create a stuffed bear, which he placed in his shop window with the name "Teddy's bear." It was an instant success, and within a year teddy bears were among the most popular toys in the United States.

Mattel was founded in 1945 in El Segundo, California, and was named for Harold "Matt" Matson and Elliot Handler. Elliot's wife, Ruth Handler, became company president and established the Barbie product line in 1959.

In 1997, **IBM**'s Deep Blue was the first machine to beat a reigning world chess champion, Garry Kasparov.

Atari, founded by Nolan Bushnell in 1972, took its name from the Japanese phrase for "prepare to be attacked." *Pong*, released by Atari, became the first commercially successful video game, selling in Sears in the 1975 Christmas season.

Parker Brothers was started in Salem, Massachusetts, in 1883. Its best-known games include Monopoly (1936), Sorry! (1934), Risk (1957), Trivial Pursuit (1979), and Ouija (1966).

Milton Bradley was established in Springfield, Massachusetts, in 1860. Its best-known games include Battleship (1967), The Game of Life (1860), and Twister (1966). In 1984, Hasbro took over Milton Bradley.

FAO Schwarz, founded in 1862, is the oldest toy store in the United States. The flagship store on Fifth Avenue in New York City has been featured in motion pictures, including *Big* (1988).

Hasbro bought **Mr. Potato Head**, its first success, from inventor George Lerner in 1952. In the 1980s Hasbro surpassed Mattel as the world's largest toy company.

Ole Kirk Chistiansen invented **Legos** in Denmark in 1932. The name *Lego* comes from the Danish term for "play well." Lego has become the world's largest tire manufacturer, creating more tires (for its Lego Building Sets) than any other company in the world.

In 1948, Richard Knerr and Arthur "Spud" Melin started **Wham-O** in their garage in Los Angeles, California. They trademarked the name Hula Hoop, an ancient toy, and they brought back another toy from ancient times, the Frisbee.

TOYS
7 POINTS

After designing the Sparrow and Hawk missile systems, engineer Jack Ryan assisted an American businesswoman, Ruth Handler, in molding **Barbie** (full name: Barbara Millicent Roberts). Barbie celebrated her fiftieth anniversary in 2009.

Mr. Potato Head was the first toy to be advertised on TV, in 1952.

Holly Hobbie is a character based on American author and illustrator Denise Holly Ulinskas. Her books inspired the dolls and the Easy Bake Oven.

In 1977, Xavier Roberts invented **Cabbage Patch Kids**, which were sold in retail stores by employees wearing hospital gowns. Cabbage

Patch Kids became the most popular gift in 1984 and were commemorated with a U.S. postage stamp in 1999.

○ ○ ○ ○ ○

Mitchell Paige was the real life inspiration for **G.I. Joe**. Snake Eyes, a
G.I. Joe character, is a mute ninja with a wolf named Timber.

○ ○ ○ ○ ○

Donald Duncan invented the **Yo-Yo** in 1929. He based the toy on a
weapon once used by Filipino hunters.

○ ○ ○ ○ ○

Silly Putty, a toy composed mainly of boric acid and silicone oil, was
introduced in the 1940s.

○ ○ ○ ○ ○

American Greetings created **Care Bears** in 1981, spawning *The Care
Bears Movie* in 1985, which became one of the highest-grossing Canadian films of all time.

○ ○ ○ ○ ○

Etch A Sketch is composed of styrene beads and aluminum. Ohio Art
created the toy in 1960.

NATIONAL TOY HALL OF FAME

The National Toy Hall of Fame, originally housed in Salem, Oregon, is now housed in the Strong National Museum of Play in Rochester, New York. The first set of inductees, announced in November 1999, include:

- Barbie
- Crayola crayons
- Erector set
- Etch A Sketch
- Frisbee
- Hula Hoop
- Legos
- Lincoln Logs
- Marbles
- Monopoly
- Play-Doh
- Radio Flyer wagon
- Roller skates
- Teddy bear
- Tinkertoys
- View-Master
- Duncan Yo-Yo

Ken Forsse created **Teddy Ruxpin** in 1985. Teddy is often sold alongside a companion toy named Grubby.

∘°○°○∘

Binney & Smith Co. created Crayola **crayons** in Easton, Pennsylvania, in 1903.

∘°○°○∘

The **Nerf** football was invented by kicker Fred Cox, who appeared in four Super Bowls with the Vikings in the 1970s. Nerf is an acronym for "non-expanding recreational foam."

Furby, the "must-have" toy from 1998, was banned by the National Security Agency of the United States due to concerns that it may be used to record and repeat classified information.

○°○°○○

Slinky was invented in 1943. The toy was flung over tree branches by soldiers in Vietnam so that it could be used as a makeshift radio antenna.

THE FINAL ROUND

CHAPTER 16

MISCELLANEOUS FACTS TO HELP YOU WIN IT ALL

Do you know . . .

- How many times Tom Cruise has been married?
- Who was named *Time* magazine's Man of the Century in 1999?
- What is the flattest U.S. state?
- Which beer won the prize for "America's Best" at the Chicago World's Fair in 1893?
- What is the only state without a rectangular flag?

Do you know the answers? These are some tough questions, so if you're not sure, bid low. Yes, I said bid low. You see, the Final Round, where you can bid 2 points all the way up to 20 points, is where every team has an equal chance . . . to blow it. Some people like to strategize their bids based on the last score update, and if you're near the top of the pack, then that's probably a smart tactic. But if you're at the bottom, the only way to score that win is to throw a Hail Mary pass, wager the full amount, and hope for the best. Everyone loves an underdog who comes from behind to win in the end. Your victory will never taste so sweet. As far as the actual questions go, hopefully you or someone on your team knows the answers. If not, do your best to narrow it down to a few choices. And if you get it wrong, try not to hold a grudge (for too long) against your friends who *insisted* they were right. The Final Round question could be anything, so here are a smattering of choices in different categories to help you prepare.

ENTERTAINMENT
2–20 POINTS

Tom Cruise, whose real name is Thomas Mapother IV, was not *Born on the Fourth of July*, but actually July 3, 1962. He's been married three times, and each wife was eleven years younger than the last. Mimi Rogers was born in 1956, Nicole Kidman in 1967, and Katie Holmes in 1978.

Tippi Hedren, the actress who played the lead in *The Birds*, is the mother of Melanie Griffith, who is the mother of Dakota Johnson, who plays a starring role in the film version of *Fifty Shades of Grey*.

The Mike Myers mask in *Halloween* was a costume mask from a 1975 film, *The Devil's Rain*, in which it was worn by **William Shatner**.

The Phantom of the Opera, which debuted on Broadway in 1988 and is produced by **Andrew Lloyd Webber**, has earned an estimated worldwide gross of more than $5.6 billion. In 2014, *The Lion King* surpassed it as the highest-grossing show of all time.

In 1927, set designer **Cedric Gibbons** designed the Academy Award, and went on to win it eleven times.

The first character to speak in the original *Star Wars Episode IV: A New Hope* is **C-3PO** (voiced by Anthony Daniels).

Merv Griffin wrote the *Jeopardy!* theme song, "A Time for Tony," as a lullaby for his son. Art Fleming was the original host in 1964 and Alex Trebek took over duties in 1984.

In 1994, *Roseanne* aired an episode called "Don't Ask, Don't Tell" that featured one of the first lesbian kisses on television.

"Yesterday" (1965), by **The Beatles,** was originally titled "Scrambled Eggs," and has become the most recorded song of all time.

Massachusetts native Katharine Lee Bates wrote the lyrics for "**America the Beautiful**" while on top of Pikes Peak, Colorado, in 1893.

Eric Clapton was the first solo performer inducted into the Rock and Roll Hall of Fame three times: for solo work, and as a member of the Yardbirds and Cream.

○°○°○○

In December 1998, **Cher**, at fifty-two years old, became the oldest woman to have a #1 single on the U.S. pop charts.

═══ PEOPLE ═══
2–20 POINTS

Richard III, the last English king to die on the battlefield, is famously quoted as saying: "A horse, a horse, my kingdom for a horse."

○°○°○○

George is the only name shared by four consecutive kings of England.

○°○°○○

William Shakespeare, the first person other than royalty to be portrayed on a British stamp (1964), was born at Stratford-upon-Avon, for which the cosmetics company Avon is named. Before the company sold cosmetics, Avon representatives used to go door-to-door selling books.

○°○°○○

James Barrie bequeathed the copyright of his most famous play, ***Peter Pan***, to London's Great Ormond Street hospital in 1929.

○°○°○○

Mark Twain took his pen name from the distance equaling two fathoms, or twelve feet.

○ ○○ ° ○ ○

Albert Einstein was named *Time* magazine's Man of the Century in 1999.

○ ○○ ° ○ ○

Dick and Mac McDonald started **McDonald's** in San Bernardino, California, in 1940. In 1961, Ray Kroc purchased the company from the brothers for $2.7 million.

○ ○○ ° ○ ○

Abraham Lincoln was shot in Ford's Theatre while watching the play *Our American Cousin*. "You sockdologizing old man-trap" (which, believe it or not, was a laugh line) were likely the last words Lincoln heard before he died. Assassin John Wilkes Booth shot Lincoln in the back of the head and then leaped onto the stage, breaking his leg before escaping.

○ ○○ ° ○ ○

Unable to say **Nelson Mandela**'s tribal name, a teacher gave him a new name, which is thought to be based on the name of British naval hero Horatio Nelson. Mandela was imprisoned from 1964 until 1990 for his participation in resistance against the South African government. The Nobel Peace Prize winner later said that meeting the Spice Girls was "one of the greatest moments of [his] life."

○ᵒ₀ᵒ○₀

In 1994, **Michael Crichton** became the only writer ever to find his works simultaneously charting at number one in television (*ER*), film (*Jurassic Park*), and books (*Disclosure*).

○ᵒ₀ᵒ○₀

Juan Ponce de León was in search of the fountain of youth when he introduced lemons and oranges to Florida. He claimed the town of St. Augustine for the Spanish crown, which is the oldest continuously European-established settlement on the continental United States.

○ᵒ₀ᵒ○₀

American poet **Maya Angelou** was San Francisco's first African American female cable car conductor.

○ᵒ₀ᵒ○₀

Tenzin Gyatso, winner of the 1989 Nobel Peace Prize, is better known as the fourteenth and current Dalai Lama, the spiritual leader of Tibet.

○ᵒ₀ᵒ○₀

Ted Kennedy was born February 22, 1932, two hundred years to the day after George Washington.

On February 28, 1997, the day associated with Monica Lewinsky's famous blue dress, President **Bill Clinton** gave her a gift of a hat pin and a copy of *Leaves of Grass* by Walt Whitman.

PLACES
2–20 POINTS

Miami was once known as "Biscayne Bay Country," and is the only major city in the United States founded by a woman, Julia Tuttle, in 1896.

Florida is America's flattest state, with a difference of only 345 feet between its highest and lowest points.

Wellington, New Zealand, is the southernmost national capital in the world. Reykjavik, Iceland, is the northernmost national capital in the world.

Kansas is the geographic center of the forty-eight contiguous states. North Dakota is the geographic center of North America.

At fifty-five miles away, **Russia** is the closest foreign nation that does not border the United States. Key West, Florida, is ninety miles from Cuba.

London is home to the world's first subway, the Tube. The oldest in the United States is the T in Boston.

Madrid is the only European national capital not situated on a river.

Pennsylvania is misspelled on the U.S. Constitution, missing the letter *n*.

Divorce is still illegal in two countries: the **Philippines** and **Vatican City**.

Only three nations have not officially adopted the metric system as their primary system of measurement: the **United States**, **Burma**, and **Liberia**.

o°o°O o

Austin, Texas, is the largest U.S. city by population that does not have a team in the MLB, NBA, NFL, or NHL.

≡ BEER ≡
2–20 POINTS

Dating back to 768, **Weihenstephan Brewery** in Bavaria is home to the oldest brewery in the world.

o°o°O o

Sapporo is Japan's oldest beer brand (1876).

o°o°O o

In the 1940s Theodor Geisel (a.k.a. Dr. Seuss) was hired by the **Narragansett Brewing Company** to create art for advertisements.

o°o°O o

Schlitz is known as "the beer that made Milwaukee famous."

o°o°O o

Pete Coors, Chairman of the **Molson Coors Brewing Company**, ran for Senate in Colorado in 2004 but lost to Ken Salazar.

o°o°O o

St. Pauli Girl beer was originally brewed next to the former St. Paul's monastery in Germany.

 ° °o°O°

President Jimmy Carter's brother, Billy Carter, promoted a beer called **Billy Beer**, which was first made in 1977. Unfortunately it only lasted roughly as long as Jimmy Carter's presidency.

 ° °o°O°

Smithwick's is an Irish red ale that has been brewed in Kilkenny, Ireland, since 1810.

 ° °o°O°

Molson began operation in Montreal in 1786. In 2005, the company merged with Coors.

 ° °o°O°

Until the 1970s, **Schaefer Beer** was the world's bestselling beer, but it ceded the title to Budweiser.

 ° °o°O°

Miller High Life is known as "the champagne of bottled beers."

 ° °o°O°

Since 1829, **Yuengling** has been brewed in Pottsville, Pennsylvania, at the oldest brewery in the United States.

∘°∘°O∘

After winning "America's Best" at the 1893 World's Columbian Exposition, also known as the Chicago World's Fair, Pabst Select changed its name to **Pabst Blue Ribbon**.

═══ FLAGS ═══
2–20 POINTS

The **Gadsden flag**, a symbol used by Benjamin Franklin, Paul Revere, and the U.S. Navy, depicts a rattlesnake with accompanying words. Both Revere's and the Navy's read, "Don't Tread On Me." Franklin's reads, "Join, or Die."

∘°∘°O∘

Ohio is the only state without a rectangular flag. Oregon is the only state with a two-sided flag.

∘°∘°O∘

Other than the American flag, the **POW/MIA** flag is the only other flag to have been flown on the moon, and at the White House.

∘°∘°O∘

The only place on U.S. soil where another flag is allowed to be hung above the "Stars and Stripes" is the **United Nations** in New York City.

∘°∘°O∘

Thirteen-year-old Native American Benny Benson designed **Alaska's state flag**, which features the Big Dipper and the North Star. Benson won a $1,000 scholarship and a watch for his efforts in 1926, but the flag's design wasn't officially adopted until 1959.

₀°₀°O₀

Hawaii's state flag has the **Union Jack** emblazoned in the upper left corner to honor the state's friendship with the British.

₀°₀°O₀

Nepal's flag is the only nonquadrilateral. Switzerland and Vatican City both have square flags.

₀°₀°O₀

Mozambique depicts an **AK-47 assault rifle** on its flag.

₀°₀°O₀

Libya's flag was solid green until 2011, when it reverted to a previous style of red, green, and black.

₀°₀°O₀

The **Southern Cross**, a constellation that can only be seen in the Southern Hemisphere, is depicted on five national flags: Australia, Brazil, New Zealand, Papua New Guinea, and Samoa.

₀°₀°O₀

Lebanon, which is the only country in the Middle East that does not have a desert, features a cedar tree on its flag.

∘ᴼ∘ᴼ∘

Paraguay is the only country with a two-sided flag.

∘ᴼ∘ᴼ∘

Red is the color most commonly found in national flags. The color purple can only be found on two flags: Spain's and Nicaragua's.

∘ᴼ∘ᴼ∘

The flag for **Antarctica** is simply a plain white map of the land mass over a light blue border.

∘ᴼ∘ᴼ∘

Though slightly different in dimensions, the flags of **Indonesia** and **Monaco** both feature the same design of a red bar above a white one. The flag of Poland features the same design, just reversed.

≡ TITANIC ≡
2–20 POINTS

Destined for New York City, after four days at sea the RMS *Titanic* struck an **iceberg** on Sunday, April 14, 1912, at 11:40 P.M. The world's then-largest ship sank two hours and forty minutes later at

2:20 A.M. Monday morning. There were 2,224 people on board, and approximately 705 survived.

∘°∘°O∘

Titanic was part of the **White Star Line**. She was the second of a series of three large ocean liners, which also included the RMS *Olympic* and the HMHS *Britannic*. *Titanic* was built in Belfast, Northern Ireland. Southampton, England, was her last English port of call, and Queenstown, now called Cobh, Ireland, was her last port of call.

∘°∘°O∘

Titanic was captained by **Edward Smith**.

∘°∘°O∘

Titanic was the first ship to use the **SOS distress signal**, a Morse code sequence developed in Germany. The ship's radio operator alternated between SOS and the more traditional CQD distress call.

∘°∘°O∘

The SS *Californian* was fifteen miles away from the crippled *Titanic* and had an adequate amount of lifeboats to rescue the ship's passengers but did not come to the rescue. The **RMS *Carpathia*** from the competing Cunard cruise line did respond and rescued 705 passengers.

∘°∘°O∘

John Jacob Astor IV, great grandson of the founder the American Fur Company, died on the *Titanic*. The U.S. investigation into the *Titanic* disaster was first held at his family's hotel, the Waldorf Astoria, in New York City.

∘°ₒ°O∘

Halifax, Nova Scotia, is home to the graves of the unclaimed bodies of those who died when the *Titanic* sank.

∘°ₒ°O∘

In September 1985, a joint French-American expedition led by Jean-Louis Michel and **Dr. Robert Ballard** found the bow and the stern of the *Titanic* on the ocean floor, nearly 2,000 feet apart.

∘°ₒ°O∘

Titanic survivor **Molly Brown**'s home became a tourist attraction in Denver, Colorado. *The Unsinkable Molly Brown* musical inspired a film, which earned Debbie Reynolds an Oscar nomination in 1964. (She lost to Julie Andrews for *Mary Poppins*.)

∘°ₒ°O∘

Titanic's band played "**Nearer, My God, to Thee**" before the ship sank.

∘°ₒ°O∘

Fenway Park and **Tiger Stadium** opened for the first time the week *Titanic* sank, both on April 20, 1912.

INDEX

A

B

S

T

ABOUT THE AUTHOR

Michael O'Neill is the founder of Pop Quiz Team Trivia, and has hosted more than 2,500 trivia games since 1997 in Greater Boston. He has amassed a database of nearly 20,000 trivia questions and facts. He lives in Brighton, Massachusetts, with his wife. For more information on Michael's trivia services, please visit: *www.mcoproductions.com*.